VALUES EDUCATION

Values Education

by Michael Silver

National Education Association
Washington, D.C.

Library of Congress Cataloging in Publication Data

Silver, Michael.
   Values education.

   (Developments in classroom instruction)
   Bibliography: p.
   1. Moral education.   I. Title.   II. Series.
   LC268.S47   370.11'4   76-29640
   ISBN 0-8106-1810-9

Acknowledgments

NEA gratefully acknowledges the permissions given to use the following:

An Anthology of Readings in Elementary Social Studies, edited by Huber M. Walsh. Copyright © 1971 by the National Council for the Social Studies. Excerpted with permission.

Becoming Aware of Values: A Resource Guide in the Use of Value Games by Bert K. Simpson. Copyright © 1972 by Pennant Press. Excerpted with permission.

"The Claim to Moral Adequacy of a Highest Stage of Moral Judgment" by Lawrence Kohlberg. *Journal of Philosophy*, Volume 70, October 25, 1973. Reprinted with permission.

Clearing House, Volume 49, March 1976. Used by permission of the Helen Dwight Reed Educational Foundation.

Controversial Issues in the Social Studies, edited by Raymond H. Muessig. Copyright © 1975 by the National Council for the Social Studies. Excerpted with permission.

"Diagnostic-Prescriptive checksheet for moral development" from "Moral Education through Diagnostic-Prescriptive Teaching Methods" by Trudi Annette Fulda and Richard Kieth Jantz. *The Elementary School Journal*, May 1975. Copyright © 1975 by The University of Chicago Press. Reprinted with permission.

Acknowledgments are continued on pages 127 and 128.

CONTENTS

Introduction

Schools are changing. In recent years there has been a remarkable resurgence of interest and emphasis on values and moral development in schools. Educators are becoming increasingly concerned over what role the schools should play in helping students to think through ethical and moral questions and to make responsible personal decisions. David Purpel and Kevin Ryan report that beyond the traditional curriculum, more and more teachers are teaching units or whole courses especially and directly aimed at moral issues.[1] Although the reasons for the increased reliance on the schools for values education remain unclear, the fact remains that the public schools currently recognize values education as within their province.

Values education can be broadly defined as the systematic effort to help students identify and develop their personal values. To educate for values is to provide opportunities for students to choose between competing values and live with the consequences of their choice. It is to enable students to gain sensitivity to values and moral issues, and to allow students to exercise their capacity for moral judgment. It also suggests providing students with abilities, skills, or strategies for clarifying values and making value judgments. All this is to say that values education incorporates many complex elements: values clarification, judgment, decision, and action.

While particular values education approaches may differ in theory, methodology, and emphasis, they have a common objective. Each approach attempts to make values and valuing serve the real needs and concerns of students. In each case, students are asked to examine their own values, emotions, and feelings, and to grapple with those of others. The following chapters focus on the process and approaches designed to foster the development of values.

1. Conceptualizing the Role of Values Education in Schools

The surge to introduce values education comes at a time when society is faced with questions arising from a breakdown of traditional values, cultural and racial conflict, and a deep distrust of the social and political institutions. The revival of what has been a major preoccupation of educators throughout history is doubtless one more indication of the confusion and anxieties of our time. As society becomes more complex and as its institutions grow and change in their nature and structure, the schools have a unique role in the development of human resources. To what needs are the schools responding? What has happened that people seek instruction in values and moral education? Why should the schools teach about values?

In recent years young people have been faced with more and more options relating to their futures, and at the same time, have been given more opportunities to make their own decisions. Many individuals are now being exposed to sexual permissiveness, increasing affluence, easy access to drugs, increased leisure time, and a long state of family dependency.[2] Rather than diminish, the future will doubtless multiply the kinds and complexities of decisions facing each individual.

In this age of alternatives and overchoice, a number of powerful forces can be identified which have contributed to the value dilemmas, the value conflicts, and the complicated decision areas that surround today's youth. They exacerbate personal conflict and decision-making by continually expanding the range and scope of value alternatives and erode confidence in the values and beliefs previously supported. Robert Barr has identified these forces as social change, media, the revolution in science and technology, and survival and environmental problems.[3] There is a need for the development of valuing skills so that youth, who are bombarded by these ideas through the media, can better judge the validity of their own values.

Add to this the concept of change brought about by overwhelming technological advance, and we have what Alvin Toffler calls "future shock."[4] Youth needs inordinate self-confidence to face drastic change, and education must play a forceful role in such attitudinal formation. Toffler writing in *Future Shock* has made this point emphatically clear: "Education's prime objective must be to increase the individual's 'cope-ability'—the speed and economy with which he can adapt to continual change."[5] Schools can assist the process of decision-making and valuing for each individual.

Values education is also partially a response to the ethical issues that seem to dominate recent social and political events. Such national issues as the war in Vietnam, the Watergate scandals, corporate bribery, and current issues, such as abortion and euthanasia, have raised fundamental questions of morality. Paul Kurtz has stated that: "Many thoughtful people today deplore what they consider to be a 'breakdown in moral values' and the form that this has taken in the younger generation."[6]

It is undoubtedly true that many adolescents and young adults often feel overpowered by forces and events in society. Students are said to be reluctant to make moral judgments and to be stressing only self-fulfillment and privacy.[7]

Because the social and personal problems within our society are rooted in value confusion, the school should play a large role in helping children to identify and clarify their values, and to make moral choices. As alienation, diversity, and individuality become the norms for society, there is a widespread feeling that American society must rediscover some common values if it is to keep from being torn apart. What bonds can schools provide to tie youth into some sort of social integration? Values education can foster integration based upon the commonly accepted values of human dignity and human worth. In an age of unprecedented moral complexity, values education can offer the nearest thing to a set of guideposts—commitment to some deeply held human values.

While the family unit has traditionally been the prime vehicle for imparting personal values and for socializing the child, many parents today are willingly allowing the schools to assist in the development of values. Citing a December, 1975, Gallup poll, *Newsweek* reports that 79 percent of the people surveyed favor "instruction in the schools that would deal with morals and moral behavior."[8] Values education can fill a vacuum left by the declining influence of parents, the churches, and other traditional sources of moral guidance.

Despite its pervasiveness and importance, a systematic approach to values development has been uncommon. Only recently has there begun to be an awareness of the need in schools for basic education in values and an awareness of the increased importance of the affective outcomes of education. Today, the affective learning that students have in their schooling experience may be the most important aspect of their education.[9]

That values education in this society has been inadequate is the conclusion of many people both inside and outside of the education field. Although little has been written about the impact of schools in transferring a valuing process to young people, probably most teachers do not deal systematically with values in their day-to-day classroom activities.[10]

Usually teachers have dealt with values in two basic ways: (1) they have tried to indoctrinate or inculcate students with "right values"—beliefs that are considered well established, generally widely accepted, and safe; or (2) they have tried to maintain a value neutrality.[11] The former alternative of teaching values has been implemented by using the "model approach" ("do as I do"), the "reward-and-punishment approach" (which encourages the repetition of desirable behavior), the "manipulative approach," and the "explanatory approach."[12]

Those teachers who give claim to value neutrality have cited the following reasons for their approach to teaching:

- Fear of indoctrinating students

- Exclusive concentration on "subject matter"

- Fear of community reaction

- A belief that value education more properly belongs with the family or church

- Ignorance as to how to proceed.[13]

11

Empirical research on the effectiveness of these approaches to values instruction is scarce. However, Merrill Harmin and Sidney Simon have long concluded that on the basis of consistent observations of young people's difficulties with values, value confusion, not value clarity, is growing in the United States.[14] Moreover, research completed by Lawrence Kohlberg of Harvard University has also demonstrated the futility of trying to inculcate values in teaching.[15] Carl Rogers has even suggested that the youth rebellion is itself the result of students' rude awakening to the confused and hypocritical value systems which they see operating in the world.[16]

Many people have spent and will continue to spend endless energy debating whether or not values education should have a role in the schools. The fact, however, is that the teaching of values is unavoidable. Values are transmitted in the educational process by the teacher's acts, comments, discussion topics, choice of books to read, homework assignments, classroom activities, and tests. They suggest to students which ideas, events, objects, and individuals their teacher considers important.

The question for educators to think about is whether they want values to develop haphazardly in students without any conscious and specific involvement on our part, or whether they intend to help students explore and come to some well-substantiated conclusions about values. The purpose of schooling is to broaden and enrich the minds and hearts of students so that they can shape their own values and arrive at their own judgments.

2. Defining Values and Value Systems

In the broadest sense, values can be defined as the preferred events that people seek. Values consist in or arise from needs and wants. But provided only with this simple definition, it would be impossible for teachers to handle adequately the kinds of difficulty in communicating with students about values. A clear understanding of human values can be gained by becoming familiar with some of the existing conceptual frameworks of values.

Milton Rokeach has provided a typology of human values.[17] According to him, a value is an enduring belief that a certain type of behavior or a certain condition of life is desirable. More specifically, he defines a value as "an enduring belief that a specific mode of conduct or end-state of existence is personally or socially preferable to an opposite or converse mode of conduct or end state of existence."[18]

Rokeach claims that human beings the world over seem to share the same small group of values, although they often disagree about which ones are the most important. Rokeach divides the 36 basic values into two categories: eighteen that apply to goals or desired-end states of human existence (terminal values) and eighteen that apply to means or desired modes of behavior (instrumental values). The values in alphabetical order are:

Terminal Values	*Instrumental Values*
A comfortable life	Ambitious
An exciting life	Broadminded
A sense of accomplishment	Capable

Terminal Values	Instrumental Values
A world at peace	Cheerful
A world of beauty	Clean
Equality	Courageous
Family security	Forgiving
Freedom	Helpful
Happiness	Honest
Inner harmony	Imaginative
Mature love	Independent
National security	Intellectual
Pleasure	Logical
Salvation	Loving
Self-respect	Obedient
Social recognition (approval)	Polite
True friendship	Responsible
Wisdom	Self-controlled

A value system is the rank-ordering of values in terms of their importance with respect to one another. A person's value system represents a learned organization of values for making choices and for resolving conflicts between values. Rokeach also claims that values are determinants of social behavior. They are the internalized standards and criteria for guiding actions, developing and maintaining attitudes, and making moral judgments.

Jack Fraenkel has expanded Rokeach's definition of values by stating that values represent what a person considers important in life. "They are ideas as to what is good, beautiful, effective, or just, and therefore worth having, worth doing, or worth striving to attain. They serve as *standards* by which we determine if a particular thing (object, idea, policy, etc.) is good or bad, desirable or undesirable, worthy or unworthy, or someplace in between these extremes."[19]

Louis Raths, Merrill Harmin, and Sidney Simon have defined a value as something of worth or worth prizing in human existence.[20] Values constitute those ideas, ideals, or beliefs by which individuals (or groups) will guide their behavior by those ideas, ideals, or beliefs. Raths, Harmin, and Simon have summarized values into three general areas: choosing, prizing, and acting. To be a value, something must be consciously considered and deliberately chosen.

Defined operationally, a value may be described as a belief, attitude, purpose, feeling, or goal that is:

1. Chosen freely

2. Chosen from alternatives

3. Chosen after thoughtful consideration of the consequences of each alternative

4. Prized

5. Publicly affirmed willingly

6. Acted upon

7. Is recurring.

"Those processes collectively define valuing. Results of the valuing process are called values."[21]

Carl Rogers has defined values by distinguishing among three uses of the term.[22] "Operative values" are employed when one makes a preferred choice for one kind of object over another. "Conceived values" are the preferences one shows for a symbolized object, ideal, or goal. "Objective values" are what is objectively preferable, "whether or not it is in fact sensed or conceived of as desirable."[23]

The work of Harold Lasswell presents a framework of universal values prized in all cultures or groups.[24] According to Lasswell, the needs and wants of an individual or a group, when determined to be desirable, or of relative worth, or of importance, become values. Lasswell believes that these eight universal values permeate the lives of all peoples, are found in all places, and have been prevalent at all times. The truly unique feature of the framework is that virtually all needs and wants of human beings can be classified under these eight value categories:

> *Respect* refers to the degree of recognition given to, or the degree of discrimination against people in their capacity as human beings; it includes concern for authority, country, peers, adults, and self.
>
> *Wealth* is the ability to provide for one's needs adequately; to develop talents that increase one's productivity to appreciate and care for material objects with which one comes into contact.
>
> *Power* refers to participation in decision-making that affects self and group values; it refers to development of leadership and followership talents.
>
> *Enlightenment* is the process of improving one's ability to make intelligent decisions in a problem-solving situation, of understanding abstractions, and mastering problem-solving techniques.
>
> *Skill* is the development of potential talents in social, communicative, physical, mental, and aesthetic areas.
>
> *Rectitude* is the degree of concern one has for the welfare of others and the degree of responsibility one has for his own conduct in association with others.

15

Well-being refers to the mental and physical health of the individual, and to his attitude toward fitness and ability to participate effectively in physical activities.

Affection is liking others, being liked, and feeling love and friendship for persons in primary and secondary relationships. In this context, primary relationships are those involving one another; secondary relationships are those between an individual and an institution or group.[25]

The Lasswell classification model is not a set of norms but a framework of open-ended continuum categories based on comprehensive cross-cultural, psychological, and historical data as well as on wide-ranging historical studies. The list of categories is, by no means, the only useful scheme for classification. It is preferred for its contextuality, economy of terms, and precision in isolating fundamentally human goals. These eight value categories provide a holistic framework within which the various social, economic, political, and personal value systems can be more clearly understood.

The Taxonomy of Educational Objectives: Handbook II—The Affective Domain by David R. Krathwohl and Benjamin S. Bloom[26] attempts to categorize behavior in the affective domain and define levels of valuing. Krathwohl and Bloom believe that children successively internalize values and develop a consistent value system. In the *Taxonomy*, values are organized along a hierarchy of levels of internalization. The levels of the domain are:

1. Receiving—(awareness of and attending to certain phenomena and stimuli)

2. Responding—(the desire and satisfaction in responding to phenomena)

3. Valuing—(acceptance of a value and commitment to it)

4. Organization—(conceptualizing and organizing a consistent value system)

5. Characterization—(integrating of beliefs, ideas, and attitudes by a value or value complex into a total philosophy or world view.)[27]

John Wilson has written extensively on moral values.[28] For Wilson moral values are basic ideas and beliefs about what is right or good and what is wrong or bad. Wilson has proposed a more complex system than simply subscribing to a set of values. He claims that the individual needs certain attributes in order to put his morality into effect. Morality is not something simply to be believed, but also something to be put into practice. Wilson sets forth six components, which can be regarded as indicating six different characteristics in the development of a person's moral abilities. Wilson gives these components Greek-derived names. They are:

- PHIL—the degree to which one can identify with other people

- EMP—insight into one's own and other people's feelings

- GIG—the mastery of adequate factual knowledge

- DIK—the rational formulation of principles concerning other people's interests

- PHRON—the rational formulation of principles concerning one's own interests

- KRAT—the ability to translate these principles into action; in a word, willpower.[29]

Lawrence Kohlberg has developed a developmental stage theory derived from his research on moral reasoning.[30] He has found developmental changes while studying individual conceptions of such universal values as life, law, roles of affection, property, contract and trust, liberty, social order and authority, and equity.[31] The six stages are:

1. Preconventional level
    At this level, the child is responsive to cultural rules and labels of good and bad, right or wrong, but interprets these labels either in terms of the physical or the hedonistic consequences of action (punishment, reward, exchange of favors) or in terms of the physical power of those who enunciate the rules and labels. The level is divided into the following two stages:
    Stage 1: *The punishment-and-obedience orientation.* The physical consequences of action determine its goodness or badness, regardless of the human meaning or value of these consequences. Avoidance of punishment and unquestioning deference to power are valued in their own right, not in terms of respect for an underlying moral order supported by punishment and authority (the latter being Stage 4).
    Stage 2: *The instrumental-relativist orientation.* Right action consists of that which instrumentally satisfies one's own needs and occasionally the needs of others. Human relations are viewed in terms like those of the marketplace. Elements of fairness, of reciprocity, and of equal sharing are present, but they are always interpreted in a physical pragmatic way. Reciprocity is a matter of "you scratch my back and I'll scratch yours," not of loyalty, gratitude, or justice.

17

II.   Conventional level

At this level, maintaining the expectations of the individual's family, group, or nation is perceived as valuable in its own right, regardless of immediate and obvious consequences. The attitude is not only one of *conformity* to personal expectations and social order, but of loyalty to it, of actively *maintaining*, supporting, and justifying the order, and of identifying with the persons or group involved in it. At this level, there are the following two stages:

Stage 3: *The interpersonal concordance or "good boy-nice girl" orientation.* Good behavior is that which pleases or helps others and is approved by them. There is much conformity to stereotypical images of what is majority or "natural" behavior. Behavior is frequently judged by intention—"he means well" becomes important for the first time. One earns approval by being "nice."

Stage 4: *The "law and order" orientation.* There is orientation toward authority, fixed rules, and the maintenance of the social order. Right behavior consists of doing one's duty, showing respect for authority, and maintaining the given social order for its own sake.

III.   Postconventional, autonomous, or principled level

At this level, there is a clear effort to define moral values and principles that have validity and application apart from the authority of the groups or persons holding these principles and apart from the individual's own identification with these groups. This level also has two stages:

Stage 5: *The social-contract, legalistic orientation,* generally with utilitarian overtones. Right action tends to be defined in terms of general individual rights and standards which have been critically examined and agreed upon by the whole society. There is a clear awareness of the relativism of personal values and opinions and a corresponding emphasis upon procedural rules for reaching consensus. Aside from what is constitutionally and democratically agreed upon, the right is a matter of personal "values" and "opinion." The result is an emphasis upon the "legal point of view," but with an emphasis upon the possibility of changing law in terms of rational considerations of social utility (rather than freezing it in terms of Stage 4 "law and order"). Outside the legal realm, free agreement and contract is the binding element of obligation. This is the "official" morality of the American government and constitution.

Stage 6: *The universal-ethical-principle orientation.* Right is defined by the decision of conscience in accord with self-chosen *ethical principles* appealing to logical comprehensiveness, universality, and consistency. These principles are abstract and ethical (the Golden Rule, the categorical imperative); they are not concrete moral rules like the Ten Commandments. At heart, these are universal principles of *justice,* of the *reciprocity* and *equality* of human *rights,* and of respect for the dignity of human beings as *individual persons.*[32]

3. Origin and Development of Children's Values

Values education focuses on the person in the learning process. The learner's values, feelings, beliefs, and judgments are of primary concern in any approach to the teaching of values. It is necessary, therefore, to ask how children acquire their values. An important area of investigation in recent years has been the development of children's values and the presence of moral judgment in children. There are several different theories which attempt to account for the origin and development of children's values. Three of the most common theoretical approaches to the study of moral development are the psychoanalytic, social-learning, and cognitive-developmental theories.

Psychoanalytic Approach

An early approach to the development of moral values occurred within the framework of psychoanalytic theory. Derived mainly from Freud's work,[33] the psychoanalytic approach conceives the development of values as a result of the establishment of the superego, a term meaning an unconscious conscience. The superego is the constellation of moral and ideal standards within the person. The function of the superego is to suppress, neutralize, or divert instincts which, if acted upon, would violate moral rules of society. It is this critical psychological mechanism that controls and directs an individual's behavior.

According to the psychoanalytic theory, the superego or conscience arises mainly from parent identification, whereby the child incorporates the values of parents into themselves. It is not until a child has truly internalized parental and societal standards that he or she will have a strong conscience, an adequately developed superego. The process of identification is exhibited by resisting temptation and arousal of guilt, anxiety, and/or shame for violating moral rules. An individual failing to act properly will feel guilty and presumably want to avoid the arousal of guilt. Virtue and capability are rewarded through enhanced self-esteem.[34] Thus, internalization of values is established during early childhood and is not affected by later identifications or influences. The process of internalization of moral values is early and final.

The psychoanalytic approach has been continued in the work of Erik Erikson.[35] Erikson has written that children develop through a series of psychological stages related to their physical maturation.[36] Erikson's stages of ego identity are segments of the life histories of individuals. They define the central concerns and conflicts of persons in a developmental period. For example, describing the first stage of ego identity, Erikson explains that children have acquired a balance of trust and distrust; trust in themselves and others, but sufficient distrust which permits the development of methods to test and assess the world they must learn to cope with. The eight stages of ego identity are:

> basic trust vs. basic mistrust
> autonomy vs. shame/doubt
> initiative vs. guilt
> industry vs. inferiority
> identity vs. role confusion
> intimacy vs. isolation
> generativity vs. stagnation
> ego integrity vs. despair.[37]

Social-Learning Approach

The main concept of social-learning theory is that values and moral behavior are learned, and that the learning processes involved do not differ in principle from those found in other sorts of behavior. Social learning as applied to moral development is based on the stimulus-response, associationist-based process of learning. The acquisition of values, or moral behavior, is learned by direct positive or negative reinforcement of behavior.

Social-learning theory is represented in the literature, most notably by the work of J. Aronfreed,[38] A. Bandura,[39] M. L. Hoffman,[40] F. J. McDonald,[41] N. E. Miller and J. Dollard,[42] Walter Mischel,[43] R. R. Sears,[44] and R. H. Walters.[45] The theory has been explained quite fully, with some important individual variations by these writers. Social-learning theorists have focused on child-rearing practices, generality of guilt, resistance to temptation, reinforcement and empathy, punishment, observation of models, and imitation.

The process of social-learning for moral development is the shaping of an individual's behavior in a desired direction. According to social-learning theories, parents play a crucial role in this process. Basically, parents shape their children's values in three ways: by punishing them, by rewarding them, and by setting an example for them.[46] Additionally, experiments have shown that behavior can be acquired through observation of models, without direct reinforcement to the observer. By identifying with a personality model which reflects given values, the child may model a parent, a teacher, a popular hero, or a peer-group member. Although preferences for certain moral values and behaviors change in relation to the child's age, cognitive understanding, and relevance to the child, social-learning theory claims that early learned behavior tends to persist.

Cognitive-Developmental Approach

The cognitive-developmental approach to higher values and judgmental processes originated in the work of Piaget,[47] and has received considerable attention in the research of Kohlberg.[48] According to cognitive-developmental theories, moral development is characterized by a number of closely interrelated functions which develop in a sequence of stages. The stage-sequence approach has the following general characteristics:

1. The stages form an invariable order or succession in which moral judgments progress

2. No stage can be skipped, for the progression occurs universally in the same order

3. The stages are qualitatively different in the sense that for any of the diverse functions, the form of functioning or operating is distinctly different from stage to stage

4. The stages are conceived of as "structured wholes" with logically consistent behaviors that appear to represent an underlying organization which characterizes each stage

5. Each stage is more complex than the preceding one, and is a hierarchial integration of the preceding stage. Thus each stage is based on and transforms the preceding stage and, at the same time, prepares for the next stage

6. Finally, progression from one stage to the next is an active process in which the child engages the environment in interactions that eventually modify cognitive structures underlying behavior.[49]

The work of Jean Piaget, presented in *The Moral Judgment of the Child*,[50] explains that moral rules are internalized (or "interiorized") to a greater or lesser degree and distinguishes three phases in development toward greater interiorization. Rules are first seen by the young child as being entirely external. Piaget describes this as heteronomous morality—the child's belief that rules originate in omniscient authority and are not subject to question. Then comes a period in which the child accepts the obligation to conform to the rules. In this stage, the child obeys the spirit, rather than simply the letter of the rule. But the rule is still something emanating from external authority.

Moral judgment does not become truly autonomous (fully interiorized) until the phase of mutual respect and cooperation is reached. At this point, the child comes to feel that he or she has agreed to be bound by certain rules of conduct for the sake of others and, in return, the others have agreed to regulate behavior for the individual's sake. Reciprocity has entered into the child's thinking. Morality at this level is said to be fully interiorized because the individual feels some control over the rules. The rules are maintained by the child's assent and not imposed by external authority. Adult constraint generally weakens as the child grows older, and much of the older child's altered way of thinking is, as described above, supposedly a consequence of his or her new-found autonomy and self-respect.

The second major theory on cognitive-moral development is that of Lawrence Kohlberg. Kohlberg has written extensively about his theory in both the professional and the popular literature, so that his three levels—preconventional, conventional, and post-conventional—and the six stages into which they are divided, two at each level, are widely known. Like Piaget, Kohlberg's explanation of moral development is much the same as it is for general cognitive development. This cognitive-developmental approach emphasizes the child's ability to reason about moral problems.

Moral development occurs as a result of role-taking experiences which present opportunities to understand the shortcomings of stages used previously. Kohlberg's theory presents moral judgment as a role-taking process, which involves taking other peoples' perspectives. Robert Selman has shown that the development of role-taking ability is a necessary condition for the acquisition of Kohlberg's conventional level of moral judgment.[51]

What is significant is Kohlberg's claim that the processes occurring in stage transition involve the person's coming to realize that certain modes of thinking are more adequate ways of handling the subject of morality. The stages are held to be successively more adequate levels of integrations in a person's moral reasoning. For example, there is the way in which rules are conceived. First they are dependent upon external compulsions and punishment, and later as instrumental to rewards (Stage 2), then as obtaining social approval (Stage 3), then as upholding some ideal order (Stage 4), and finally as articulations of social principles necessary for living together with others (Stages 5 and 6, principled morality). The form of reasoning then (as distinguished from the content of rules) is universal, as is the invariant sequence of stages.[52]

Some additional contributions of Kohlberg's research into cognitive moral development have been succinctly described by Edwin Fenton.[53] Major findings mentioned are as follows:

I.   People think about moral issues in six qualitatively different stages arranged in three levels of two stages each.

II.   The most reliable way to determine a stage of moral thought is through a moral interview.

III.   A stage is an organized system of thought.

IV.   An individual reasons predominately at one stage of thought and uses contiguous stages as a secondary thinking pattern.

V.   These stages are natural steps in ethical development, not something contrived or invented.

VI.   All people move through these stages in invariant sequence, although any individual may stop at a particular stage.

VII. People can understand moral arguments at their own stage, at all stages beneath their own, and usually at one stage higher than their own.

VIII. Higher moral stages are better than lower ones.

IX. Stage transition takes place primarily because encountering real life or hypothetical moral dilemmas sets up cognitive conflict in a person's mind and makes the person uncomfortable.

X. Deliberate attempts to facilitate stage change through educational programs in schools have been successful.

XI. Moral judgment is a necessary but not sufficient condition for moral action.

4. Role of the Teacher in Values Education

Teachers have an important and difficult role to play in the process of values teaching. "What teachers do in their dealings with students influence the values of those students."[54] The proper role of the teacher in values education can vary considerably according to the distinctiveness of the individual. The teacher does, however, have two very important responsibilities in the development of values. First, the teacher must be him or herself, and secondly, the teacher must let the students be themselves.[55] The teacher's role is, not to teach values per se, but rather to guide each child toward clarifying his or her personal values, to deal with value conflicts, and to become aware of those factors which are related to the values of others. To be sure, the role of the teacher in establishing an atmosphere and climate for discussing values is critical.

Classroom Atmosphere and Climate

Robert Soar has found, as a result of his studies of teacher-student interaction, that the environment which the teacher creates through his or her classroom management is extremely influential in determining the values that the children will eventually embrace.[56] In setting the atmosphere and climate that foster the pursuit of values, the teacher needs to provide a climate of openness to ideas and freedom of expression. Students should be allowed the free and independent determination of their own personal values.

One of the most important elements in building such a climate is trust. Richard and Gerri Curwin have described a three-stage process to enable the teacher to establish a trusting relationship among the students and between students and teacher.[57] The stages are: (1) acceptance of students' responses, (2) willingness to take risks, and (3) openness in sharing thoughts and feelings.

Raths, Simon, and Harmin have suggested that values education is most successful in a psychologically safe classroom environment.[58] In a safe climate students feel accepted, supported, relaxed, and generally unthreatened. To build a safe atmosphere the teacher should offer warm support to all students and exhibit a genuine concern for them. The teacher should attempt to understand the students' positions on classroom issues and incorporate them into decisions that are made.

Ryals and Foster state that values education can be most successfully managed in a classroom atmosphere where students feel they have free choice.[59] "Free choice demands a respect for the rights of a decision-maker to select a course of action that may be in opposition to both majority sentiment and teacher wants."[60] The kinds of free choice described here are intended to encourage the development of a classroom climate where students not only experience choice but also the consequences of choosing. Values development occurs as students choose from among several possible alternative values and consider their consequences. Leland W. Howe and Mary Martha Howe suggest that teachers should provide some measure of choice to indicate their confidence in the students' ability to make decisions about their own learning.[61]

Lawrence Kohlberg has also maintained that moral development is more likely to be stimulated in classrooms that are just and democratic, where mutual respect is in evidence, and where opportunities for choice exist.[62] He has maintained that a child will more likely advance through the stages of moral development in classrooms that are managed with fair and reasonable concern for the interests of everyone.

To support a classroom climate characterized by acceptance, trust, and choice is not to advocate a permissive classroom. Permissiveness is not what is needed. "What is needed is that the teacher treat students as other people, who have a diversity of abilities and desires (just as he has), and with whom he happens to be engaged in certain semi-personal cooperation activities."[63] When the teacher shows respect for the student as a person, then "the classroom can become a place with an atmosphere of mutual respect in which students can doubt, risk, raise new questions, challenge old beliefs, and struggle with moral reasoning."[64]

Conducting Classroom Discussions

It has been discovered that teachers of different personality types and teaching styles can effectively promote the open discussion of values. "Classroom effectiveness seems directly related to the teacher's ability to respect student ideas and accept student value positions."[65]

The process of discussing value issues should avoid moralizing, criticism, insistence on teaching personal values, or evaluating ideas presented by students as good, bad, or acceptable. Whatever is said by the student should be accepted by the teacher with no sign of condemnation, rejection, or ridicule. The task of not commenting or of controlling one's facial expression is often difficult. Yet, while the teacher should be non-judgmental, it is important for the teacher to be concerned with the ideas expressed by students.

Discussion should encourage expression of individuality. The teacher should try to maintain a classroom atmosphere conducive to open discussion and exercise care that the class is not unfairly balanced one way or another. All students should have the opportunity to express their feelings on different topics, as well as the right to expect that their thoughts will be respected by their fellow classmates. Students should be taught to accept the thoughts of others in a supportive manner. In any discussion, each individual should have the right to "pass"—to refuse to speak if the expression of a thought is too painful. The teacher should rarely force anyone to participate. Value positions will not be expressed unless discussions are democratic, without pressures to conform, with freedom to state thoughts, and with the right to disagree. Value statements may be seen as alternatives rather than correct answers. The result should be an atmosphere of acceptance wherein students feel safe even though their ideas are not universally accepted. Finally, the purpose of the discussion should not be to arrive at a single answer to a problem. The teacher should work to keep the issues open rather than to seek consensus.

Opportunities for discussing value questions can occur in several ways: those opportunities that are planned and structured and initiated by the teacher; those times when value issues or questions are anticipated and may or may not occur; and those spontaneous occurrences which arise out of some classroom incident or unanticipated discussion. Teachers will want to be prepared to address value questions whenever they occur. In this case, especially, teachers will want to be aware of their personal value system, which is inevitably revealed through their actions and concerns.

Bernice Wolfson has provided a good illustration of this process:

> An observer in a classroom can infer what appear to be the values of the teacher, i.e., what is prized, important, of greatest concern. If, on the one hand, she scolds and embarrasses a child before the whole class because he has broken a large jar of paste, it would appear that she values this property more than the feelings of this child. If she tears up a child's paper because it is not neat, she appears to be valuing her standard of neatness over the child's effort and feelings.[66]

While it is important for teachers to participate and share in values discussions, teachers must be careful to offer their own alternatives simply as other opinions for consideration. It is often too easy for teachers to impose their values and beliefs upon children through personal authority, personal judgments, or personal points of view.

In the eyes of students, a great deal of status and authority is associated with a teacher. The role of the teacher should not be to influence students unduly with what the teacher thinks about an issue. Two suggestions may be helpful here: (1) In the course of a discussion, do not make substantive statements—only ask questions, and (2) do not give your judgment or opinion until the end.[67] If the teacher waits until after students have an opportunity to think about an issue, students will not be as tempted to accept the teacher's position.

Selecting Topics and Issues

One of the ways in which teachers can help students in valuing is to raise values questions and allow for discussion. Students should be given opportunities to investigate and discuss value questions and should be allowed to make up their minds about these vital matters without being unduly influenced by the teacher.[68]

One approach in selecting issues in values education is to select topics as they appear in the subject matter.[69] Literature, history, and social studies are filled with moral and value issues. The selection of value topics can focus on personal and social moral dilemmas, and the reasons individuals give for resolving them. A related method of selection would be to obtain a commercially prepared curriculum. Many such materials and packages are described in the Bibliography. Either approach allows for pre-planning of both the sequence and the content of value issues.

An alternative method of selection is to identify some substantive value issues and questions according to children's age and maturity levels. This would allow for planning so that value questions would come up at a time and in a way that children and teachers can learn to handle them. An example of this approach is offered by Clive Beck.[70] Beck has identified a variety of "substantive" topics which are appropriate for values education content beginning with 5–9 years of age and continuing through ages 16–18. The topics he has suggested for 5–9-year-olds include:

- Helping other people

- The self and others

- The value of rules to ourselves and others

- Exceptions to rules

- The need to look ahead

- Parent-child relationships

- Attitudes toward teachers

- Other authorities in society

- The need to learn

- The need for advice

- Making up one's mind

- Valuable goals in life

- The legitimacy of happiness as a goal

- The place of work.

With respect to topics for ages 10 and 11, Beck has suggested the following under the heading of "human relations":

- Rules people give up

- The place of rules in society

- Exceptions to society's rules

- The individual's need for other people

- Helping other people

- The self and others

- The place of laws, judges, and police

- The place of governments and other authorities

- Lawbreaking and the place of punishment

- Different values and rules in our society

- Different values and rules around the world

- Loyalty and patriotism

- The place of the inner group of relatives and friends

- Parent-child relationships

- Prejudice against races, social classes, and other groups

- Differences in taste in our society and around the world.

The topics for ages 12 and 13 are focused on decision-making. Among the topics are:

- Worthwhile goals to pursue in life

- The place of education in one's life

- Work and leisure

- The place of leisure, recreation, and exercise

- Alcohol and drugs

- Vocational decision-making

- Personal moral virtues

- The need to look ahead.

For ages 14 and 15, Beck has suggested a number of topics which have to do with contemporary social problems such as:

- War

- Disarmament

- Underdeveloped nations

- Pollution

- Population control

- Abortion

- Euthanasia

- Nationalism

- Racism

- Women's liberation.

Finally, for ages 16–18, Beck has suggested a range of topics concerned with consideration of general value theory that includes the following:

- The purpose of morality

- Justifying moral judgments

- The self and others

- Favoring an inner group

- Human moral psychology

- Attaining moral maturity

- Hedonistic and utilitarian theories

- Principles of decision-making.

Many of the topics and issues which are ripe for values and moral discussions originate within the classroom. The discussion of classroom rules, for example, and incidents which occur in the classroom can be potent value issues. More important, however, are the student's own concerns, interests, and goals as a primary basis for values instruction.[71] The genuine personal and social issues which are experienced by students themselves can provide meaningful dialogue for values and moral development.[72]

In addition to discussion, there are other kinds of experiences that can help children to experience valuing and engage in decision-making. These activities include: experiencing the feelings and dilemmas of literary characters, participating in creative dramatics or role-playing, examining some of the personal concerns or problems that grow out of school life, and writing personal sketches about themselves, perhaps in a journal.

31

32

Student Process

Teaching Skill

Cluster 3

Encouraging
Alternative
Behaviors

| Exploring Alternative Behaviors |

Cluster 2

Clarifying Pupils'
Expressions of Feelings
and Values

| Reflecting Pupils' Feelings | | Asking Clarifying Questions | | Identifying Discrepancies |

Cluster 1

Eliciting Pupils'
Expressions of Feelings
and Values

| Attending Behavior | | Initiating the Affective Situation | | Asking Inventory Questions | | Reinforcing Pupils' Expressions of Feelings and Values |

FIG. 1—"Taxonomy of interpersonal skills," from "Microteaching for Affective Skills," by Mary and David Sadker, *The Elementary School Journal*, November, 1975. p. 94.

Helping Students in Valuing and Decision-Making

"Values and valuing are personal, often gradual accommodations to new ideas, attitudes, and beliefs."[73] They grow out of personal experience and develop and change over the course of a lifetime. The process of valuing and decision-making encourages students to acquire values by making choices, through prizing one over another, through rejecting one and adhering to another, and through clarifying issues related to values. To teach the valuing process is to provide students with value alternatives to analyze and explore for themselves.

> According to this plan, a student would be taught to identify or face up to the particular values he is living in his life here and now; to analyze these values in terms of their meaning for him as an individual and for the others around him; and to live in consistency with the values he holds.[74]

The valuing process also suggests providing students with abilities, skills, or strategies for conducting values analysis in their own lives. J. P. Shaver and W. Strong have identified cognitive and affective components of valuing to arrive at an integrated teaching approach.[75] The components of valuing include: values identification and clarification, label generalization, examination of consequences, value conflict and resolution, and value commitment. Shaver and Strong believe that the teacher's role in valuing is to assist each student to develop a rational foundation for his or her own values, and to acquire the related analytical concepts to use after leaving school.[76]

Myra and David Sadker have organized a taxonomy of teaching skills which are necessary to help students in valuing.[77] (See Figure 1.) These skills are grouped into three clusters: The first cluster of skills is designed to help the teacher elicit students' expressions of feelings and values. The skills in the second cluster help the teacher clarify students' values and affective comments. And the skills in the third cluster attempt to encourage students to explore alternative behaviors which are consistent with expressed feelings and values.

According to the Sadkers, the skills which are necessary to open a dialogue on a values issue (cluster one) consists of direct-eye contact and physical posture toward the student as well as facial and verbal cues which indicate that the teacher is attentive and encouraging. Other skills designed to encourage students to express feelings and values include: (1) an appropriate seating arrangement, (2) the use of questions which make students aware of their feelings, thoughts, and behaviors (3) the rewarding of students' willingness to share feelings and values, and (4) the teacher's desire to share his or her own feelings and values.

The following skills are to help students clarify their value statements elicited in cluster one. These skills are: (1) identifying the students' feelings and emotions based on their comments, (2) paraphrasing or responding to those comments, (3) posing questions to help students analyze and clarify their feelings and values, and (4) identifying discrepancies between students' values and behavior, between values and data, and between self-perception and others' perceptions.

The final cluster area is composed of one skill—encouraging students to explore alternative behaviors. The teacher can provide opportunities for students to try out new behaviors, structure situations in which students can try out these behaviors, and arrange for evaluation of results.

The role of the teacher in helping students in valuing is to recognize that within each student there exists an array of values that influence the way the student acts and reacts in a given situation.

> The verbalizations of students are often expressions of values emanating from their self-structures. As the teacher responds to his students, he responds to an interwoven pattern of self and values. A sensitivity to the students' values enables the teacher to become more closely attuned to the students' essence as a person. . . . The valuing teacher possesses a caring attitude that is so deeply a part of him that it can be sensed and responded to by those students with whom he is in contact. It is this caring attitude which is often the difference between effective and ineffective teaching.[78]

5. Various Approaches to Teaching Values

There are seven important approaches to values instruction: (1) Values Clarification, (2) Values Inculcation, (3) Moral Reasoning and Cognitive Moral Development, (4) Values Analysis, (5) Role Playing for Social Values, (6) Confluent Education, and (7) Action Learning. Each approach involves a different means of values development, although advocates for each claim that individual value decisions will be more soundly based, more coherently made, and more consistently acted upon through their approach. Generally, advocates for each of the approaches have claimed that as a result of exposure to deliberate values education, children will be able to cope more adequately with their value judgments and moral positions.

Values Clarification

Raths, Harmin, and Simon have formulated values clarification to help individuals clarify their values.[79] Values clarification enables individuals to decide what it is they themselves wish to prize in life. According to the developers of values clarification, individuals should create their own value systems, and any approach which attempts to impose values is both unethical and unsound. The goal then is to make a conscious attempt to avoid all forms of moralizing and, in so far as possible, to eliminate expression of the teacher's bias. The emphasis is on individual freedom, healthy spontaneous growth, and respect for the values of other people, societies, and cultures.

Values clarification attempts to focus the curriculum on values by systematically encouraging students to engage actively in activities that will aid them in formulating and clarifying their own values. Values clarification should encompass the levels of facts, concepts, and values, and its ultimate goal should be to help a person "discover cognitive and personal meaning for himself."[80] The teacher is permitted to express his or her own views, but only as an example of one way to look at things, and not as a right answer.

The authors of values clarification have delineated seven operations which they call a "process of valuing." Individuals must go through each operation before they can say that they have derived a value. The processes are:

CHOOSING	(1)	freely
	(2)	from alternatives
	(3)	after thoughtful consideration of the consequences of each alternative
PRIZING	(4)	cherishing, being happy with the choice
	(5)	willing to affirm the choice publicly
ACTING	(6)	doing something with the choices
	(7)	repeatedly in some pattern of life.[81]

The term *value indicator* is an important concept in values clarification. A value indicator is simply something that is not a value as it does not meet all seven criteria under the value definition. A value indicator shows a person what values that person is in the process of forming. As a consequence, it is very significant in the values-clarification process. Value indicators have been described as goals or purposes, aspirations, attitudes, interests, feelings, beliefs and convictions, activities, and worries, problems, and obstacles.[82]

The values-clarification method is essentially inductive, moving from specific group experience to general ideas about self-knowledge and self-awareness. By drawing on their resources, students attempt to come to terms with the task of values clarification while increasing their understanding of themselves. Students are also able to compare their own perceptions and experiences with those of other group members. Values clarification offers a process—not a set of values all students should hold.

The role of the teacher in values clarification is to assist students in becoming aware of their own value positions. The teaching process involves several essential elements. First, the teacher must make efforts to elicit attitudinal and value statements from students. Secondly, the teacher must accept the thoughts, feelings, beliefs, and ideas of students, nonjudgmentally, without trying to change them or criticize them. Thirdly, the teacher must raise questions with students which help them think about their values.

The basic strategy for helping students clarify their own values is the "clarifying response." Clarifying responses are questions which are asked orally or written on student papers. Raths, Simon, and Harmin have suggested such questions as—

- Where do you suppose you first got that idea?

- What else did you consider before you picked this?

- What would be the consequences of each alternative available?

- Are you glad you feel that way?

- Would you tell the class the way you feel sometime?

- I hear what you are for; now is there anything you can do about it? Can I help?

- Have you felt this way for some time?[83]

These questions are linked to the seven-step process of arriving at a value.

Values clarification uses a series of group exercises—called strategies—through which participants experience some important and personal aspects of conflicting or confusing values. Some typical areas of value conflict or confusion are: politics, religion, work, leisure time, school, love, sex, family, material possessions, culture, personal tastes, friends, money, aging, death, health, race, war-peace, rules, and authority.[84] Each exercise is then processed individually or by the group. This is where actual learning takes place. Through the teacher, who is really a facilitator in creating the proper atmosphere, the student continually develops a process of valuing, i.e., of making decisions solely on what he or she prizes and cherishes in life. Four such strategies are described below.

"NAME TAG"[85]

Purpose: This strategy asks participants to look more closely at what they value and what they are. Secondly, it asks them to publicly affirm these aspects of themselves by having students tell something about who they are.

Directions: Group members are asked to make 5 × 7 name cards, placing their first name in the middle of the card. The teacher then asks students to answer questions and write their responses in the various corners of the card.

Upper right hand corner: Give the names of three people in public life whom you most admire. Give the names of three people in public life whom you least admire.

Middle right: Describe three qualities or characteristics which you would like to possess.

Lower right hand corner: Draw a picture of how you feel right now. You may use any object as a symbol of your feelings.

Upper left hand corner: List three qualities other people would use to describe you.

Middle left: List three qualities you would use to describe yourself.

Lower left hand corner: Briefly describe how you feel today using weather report terminology. (sunny, cloudy, etc.)

Bottom center: State something about which you feel strongly against.

Following the completion of the name card, the teacher asks everyone to stand up and mill about the room in random fashion, reading each other's name tags and asking questions if they feel like it.

"VALUES VOTING"[86]

Purpose: This is a strategy that allows students to indicate their feelings and thoughts publicly on any questions asked of them, and to see how others feel about the same things. It emphasizes that people differ. This is a time when students can give answers without being told that they are right or wrong. All opinions on any issue are respected.

Directions: The teacher explains that a vote will be taken on a number of questions, and each student will show how he or she feels or thinks about the subject by doing the following: positive answer—raise hands; negative answer—thumbs down; neutral or pass—fold arms. If the student feels strongly about the subject, this is indicated by vigorous hand waving as the case may be. After the questions have been posed, the teacher can ask several students to share their feelings about a particular question and give reasons for voting as they did. Those questions where big differences occur can lead to good class discussions. Each of the questions are prefaced with "How many of you . . . ?" Some examples of questions follow on the next page:

How many of you think teenagers should be allowed to choose their own clothes?

How many of you will raise your children more strictly than you were raised?

How many of you watch TV more than three hours per day?

How many of you think the most qualified person usually wins in school elections?

How many of you think there are times when cheating is justified?

"TWENTY THINGS YOU LOVE TO DO"[87]

Purpose: This exercise attempts to help students look at themselves and their behavior in order to clarify their values. Students are given some insight into what is important to them by examining their own patterns of behavior and consistency in actions.

Directions: Students are asked to write down twenty things they like to do. Next, students are asked to code their list using the right-hand columns of their paper. They can put the suggested symbol at the top of each column and proceed to fill out each row according to the following directions.

Symbol	Directions
A/P	Put an A for activities you prefer doing alone, P for activities you prefer doing with people.
$3	Check each activity that costs more than $3.
Pub	Check each activity that you would be willing to declare publicly.
2 yrs	Check those you would list two years ago.
F	Check those your father would put on his list.
M	Check those your mother would put on her list.
Date	Write the approximate date you last did each activity.
0	How often this year did you do it (never, seldom, often, very often)?
Rank	Number the top five (1–5), the ones you like to do best.

Ask students to review their lists and to write what they learned about themselves. Students are to look at this coded data in the way a natural scientist would. What can the student spot as trends, patterns, or threats? What does the data suggest?

"A PERSONAL COAT OF ARMS"[88]

Purpose: This strategy is designed to help students learn more about their most strongly held values and to learn the importance of publicly affirming what they believe in.

Directions: Each student is asked to draw a shield shaped in preparation for making a personal coat of arms. The shield is divided into six sections. The teacher makes it clear that words are to be used only in the sixth block. All the others are to contain pictures. The following is placed into each section:

1. Draw two pictures, one to represent something you are very good at and one to show something you want to become good at.

2. Make a picture to show one of your values from which you would never budge. This is one about which you feel extremely strong and which you might never give up.

3. Draw a picture to show a value by which your family lives. Make it the one that everyone in your family would probably agree is the most important.

4. In this block, imagine that you could achieve anything you wanted, and whatever you tried to do would be a success. What would you strive to do?

5. Use this block to show one of the values you wished all people would accept, and certainly one in which you believe very deeply.

6. In the last block, you can use words. Use four words which you would like people to say about you behind your back.

SELECTED BIBLIOGRAPHY OF SUPPORTING CURRICULUM MATERIALS FOR VALUES CLARIFICATION

Bellanca, James A. *Values and the Search for Self*. Wash., D.C.: National Education Association, 1975.

Personal values clarification is placed on areas of teaching such as exercising personal control, assessing needs, setting up goals, using resources, and evaluating outcomes.

Bolton, Robert. *Values Clarification for Educators.* Cazenovia, N.Y.: Ridge Consultants, 1974.

Provides some theory and guidelines, helpful to those who wish to practice values clarification.

_____. *Workbook in Values Clarification.* Cazenovia, N.Y.: Ridge Consultants, 1974.

Describes methods and strategies of values clarification with different age groups.

Casteel, J. Doyle, and Stahl, Robert J. *Value Clarification in the Classroom: A Primer.* Pacific Palisades, Calif.: Goodyear Publishing Co. Inc., 1975.

Designed to be used in undergraduate, graduate, and in-service teacher education courses. It is intended to enable teachers to facilitate student behaviors associated with values clarification.

Cole, Richard A. *A New Role for Geographic Education: Values and Environmental Concerns.* Oak Park, Ill.: National Council for Geographic Education, 1974.

A values-clarification approach to teaching geography.

Curwin, Gerri, and others. *Search for Values.* Dayton, Ohio: Pflaum/Standard, 1972.

This kit contains 44 lessons designed to help high school students clarify their personal values in relation to the topics of time, competition, authority, personal space, commitment, relationship, and images.

Curwin, Richard L.; Curwin, Gerri; and editors of *Learning* magazine. *Developing Individual Values in the Classroom.* Palo Alto, Calif.: Learning Handbooks Education Co., 1974.

A practical guidebook which provides activities, teaching strategies, and procedures to help students examine and clarify values.

Elder, Carl A. *Making Value Judgments: Decisions for Today.* Columbus, Ohio: Charles E. Merrill Publishing Co., 1972.

Uses an inquiry-values analysis approach. Students are also asked to make choices from alternatives, consider the consequences, and use the chosen values for themselves as a basis for action. (Teachers manual.)

Flynn, Elizabeth N., and LaFaso, John F. *Designs in Affective Education: A Teacher Resource Program for Junior and Senior High.* New York: Paulist Press, 1974.

A major resource offering teachers strategies for use in a variety of educational settings including the areas of values clarification, intercultural education, violence, prejudice, ecology, city planning, and drug education.

Hall, Brian P. *Values Clarification as Learning Process—A Guidebook.* New York: Paulist Press, 1973.

A basic manual of projects and exercises to help participants examine and clarify their values. Included are definitions of values and value indicators, value techniques, classroom techniques, and designs for conferences of values clarification.

_____. *Values Clarification as Learning Process—A Handbook for Christian Educators.* New York: Paulist Press, 1973.

A guide to the effective use of values clarification in religious education settings. Examines the priority of values, the theoretical bases of the methodology, with application for parish renewal, liturgy, and prayer life.

_____. *Values Clarification as Learning Process—A Sourcebook.* New York: Paulist Press, 1973.

Examines values and how people use or misuse them in their personal lives. This book contains a variety of practical techniques designed to engage the reader in the process of clarifying his or her own values.

Harmin, Merrill. *Got To Be Me! A Personal Identity and Self-Awareness Program for Younger Elementary Students.* Niles, Ill.: Argus, 1976.

Primary-Intermediate self-expression, self-awareness program consists of stimulus cards which contain unfinished sentences.

_____. *Making Sense of Our Lives.* Niles, Ill.: Argus, 1974.

Containing three kits, this multimedia program provides experiences to help students clarify their values: to make thoughtful choices in real-life situations, listen to others, and express personal convictions with confidence.

_____. *People Projects.* Menlo Park, Calif.: Addison-Wesley, 1973.

The project cards in this program are designed to help students think about personal events, find satisfactory thoughts in such thinking, clarify their confusions and inconsistencies, appreciate others' experiences, and develop small group skills, abilities for responsible self-direction, and mature value thinking.

Harmin, Merrill; Simon, Sidney B.; and Kirschenbaum, Howard. *Clarifying Values Through Subject Matter.* Minneapolis: Winston Press, 1973.

A three-level theory of subject matter and examples of how every subject in the curriculum can be taught with a focus on values clarification.

Hawley, Robert. *Human Values in the Classroom: Teaching for Personal and Social Growth.* Amherst, Mass.: Education Research Associates, 1973.

Sets forth a basic approach to teaching and learning based on specific processes—orientation, community building, achievement motivation, fostering open communication, information processes, values exploration, and planning for change.

Hawley, Robert C. *Value Exploration Through Role-Playing* (Practical Strategies for Use in the Classroom). New York: Hart Publishing Co., 1975.

Role-playing techniques are applied in teaching subject matter, moral judgment, and decision-making.

Hawley, Robert, and Hawley, Isabel. *Developing Human Potential: A Handbook of Activities for Personal and Social Growth.* Amherst, Mass.: Education Research Associates, 1975.

Activities are divided in six areas: motivation, self-awareness, communication skills, interpersonal relationships, creativity, and teaching academic subjects.

―――――――――. *A Handbook of Personal Growth Activities for Classroom Use.* Amherst, Mass.: Education Research Associates, 1972.

Provides practical activities to help students improve their self-awareness and ability to interact with others.

―――――――――. *Human Values in the Classroom: A Handbook for Teachers.* New York: Hart Publishing Co., 1975.

Many techniques and classroom procedures are introduced, including values exploration, values clarification, and decision-making.

Hawley, Robert C.; Simon, Sidney B.; and Britton, D. D. *Composition for Personal Growth: Values Clarification Through Writing.* New York: Hart Publishing Co., 1973.

Numerous strategies for stimulating creative writing. Designed primarily for English teachers, but can be adapted for other areas.

Howe, Leland W., and Howe, Mary Martha. *Personalizing Education: Values Clarification and Beyond.* New York: Hart Publishing Co., 1975.

A handbook of practical ways to make values clarification and other affective techniques an integral part of the classroom. Specific techniques for personalizing are developed for (1) human relationships, (2) goals in the classroom, (3) the curriculum, and (4) classroom organization and management.

Klein, Ronald, and others. *Search for Meaning.* Dayton, Ohio: Pflaum/Standard, 1974.

The 36 lessons in this junior high program are designed to provide students with opportunities to reflect on their lives and to clarify their personal values in relation to external forces, internal drives, and relationships with others.

Miguel, Richard J. *Decision: A Values Approach to Decision-Making.* Columbus, Ohio: Charles E. Merrill, 1974.

The components of the multimedia kit include activity cards, spirit masters, sound filmstrip, cassette, resource materials, and handbook to aid in the values-clarification process.

Paulson, Wayne. *Deciding for Myself: A Values Clarification Series.* Minneapolis: Winston Press, 1974.

A series of four sets of short booklets with over 150 values-clarifying strategies and activities.
Set A-Clarifying My Values
Set B-My Everyday Choices
Set C-Where Do I Stand
Set D-Exploring Traditional Values Relevant to the Bicentennial
An extensive teacher's guide explains the theory and several techniques of values clarification and offers specific guidelines for sequencing and structuring the use of the clarifying strategies. Grades 6–12.

Raths, Louis; Harmin, Merrill; and Simon, Sidney B. *Values and Teaching.* Columbus, Ohio: Charles E. Merrill Publishing Co., 1966.

The basic text and original book on values clarification. Includes the theory, answers to many questions on classroom use, and 20 specific strategies, including chapters on the clarifying response and values sheets.

Searching for Values: A Film Anthology. New York: Learning Corporation of America, 1972.

Fifteen motion pictures, edited for classroom use, which provoke students to recognize and question their own values, attitudes, and goals, those of society, and of other cultures.

Simon, Sidney B. *The IALAC Story: A Modern Allegory on the Classical Putdown.* Niles, Ill.: Argus Press, 1973.

Also available with filmstrip.

_____. *Meeting Yourself Halfway.* Niles, Ill.: Argus Communications, 1974.

Gives teachers and students strategies for looking at and assessing their lives. The 31 activities are intended for personal or group use.

_____. *Values Clarification: Friends and Other People.* Arlington Heights, Ill.: Paxcom Communications, Inc., 1973.

A multimedia unit for teaching values clarification. Included are six films, students' worksheets, student journals, and teacher's manual.

Simon, Sidney B., and Clark, Jay. *Beginning Values Clarification: A Guidebook for the Use of Values Clarification in the Classroom.* San Diego: Pennant Educational Materials, 1975.

Extends values clarification by presenting new strategies especially suited for helping teenagers and young adults clarify their values.

Simon, Sidney B.; Howe, Leland; and Kirschenbaum, Howard. *Values Clarification: A Handbook of Practical Strategies for Teachers and Students.* New York: Hart Publishing Co., 1972.

Detailed instructions for 79 values clarification strategies with many examples for the basic strategies.

Simon, Sidney B., and Kirschenbaum, Howard. *Readings in Values Clarification.* Minneapolis: Winston Press, 1973.

Numerous articles on values clarification and other phases of values education by such noted authors as John Holt, Carl Rogers, and Sidney Simon. Includes chapters on values and subject matter, values and the family, and values in religious education.

Simon, Sidney B.; Kirschenbaum, Howard; and Fuhrmann, Barbara. *An Introduction to Values Clarification.* New York: J. C. Penny Company, 1972.

A teaching kit on values clarification containing a seven-part unit.

Valett, Robert. *Self-Actualization.* Niles, Ill.: Argus Communications, 1974.

Helpful in clarifying values, and forming and evaluating life styles.

Van Scotter, Richard D., and Cauley, Jon. "Future Values for Today's Curriculum." *Scholastic Teacher*, February 1974. pp. 18–22.

Applies an inquiry and clarification approach to teaching about future values.

Williams, Elmer. *Social Studies for the Elementary School Proficiency Model #5, Values and the Valuing Process.* Athens: University of Georgia, 1972.

This is a teacher training module designed to help teachers develop competency in using values-clarification strategies.

Values Inculcation

Values inculcation has been explained by Douglas P. Superka as an approach to instill or internalize certain desired values into students.[89] He states that within inculcation ". . . values are viewed as standards or rules of behavior the source of which is society or culture."[90] Thus, the process of acquiring values is that of identification with a person, group, or society.

Several teaching methods of inculcating values that can be accomplished directly or indirectly have already been identified. These include: modeling, positive and negative reinforcement, explanation, and manipulation. The modeling approach is one of acquainting students with examples of exemplary behavior and desirable values. Instances of modeling behavior may be drawn from history, literature, legend or, more directly, from examples set by teachers and students. The reward and punishment approach encourages the repetition of desirable behavior. Here, it is assumed that when students are punished for infractions of rules and praised for obedience, they will take on the values associated with the desired behavior. The manipulation approach is exercised as teachers would manipulate the environment or the experiences to which students are exposed, so as to favor certain value outcomes. Finally, perhaps the most common approach to inculcation is to provide explanations for values that are to be promoted. Teachers always seem ready to tell students what they should believe and how they should act.

As explained earlier in the chapter on "Value Systems," the Lasswell Value Framework is built around the early work of Harold Lasswell. He has determined that there are eight universal values, needs, wants, and aspirations prized in any culture or group. These values are necessary for all human beings. Persons deprived of any one or more of these eight value categories will have difficulty in any society. The value categories are respect, wealth, power, enlightenment, skill, rectitude, well-being, and affection.

These eight all-inclusive value categories have been adapted for educational use by W. R. Rucker, V. C. Arnspiger, and A. Brodbeck,[91] and others.[92] Rucker, et al., focus on the eight value categories to develop an organized framework for communicating with students about values. The essence of their work is based on the philosophy that the role of the school in shaping and sharing human values is imperative in a democracy.

The process of building those positive values that contribute to the value-sharing process concept of a democratic society is labeled *value enhancement,* while those actions and/or activities that act to withhold or inhibit the realization of any value are considered *value deprivations.*

The goals for developing values within the school classroom have been described as follows:

1. The objective of school is realization of human worth in both theory and fact.

2. The school which is oriented toward human dignity is one in which human values are widely shaped and shared.

3. In such a school the formation of mature personalities whose

value demands and capabilities are compatible with this ideal is essential.

4. The long-range goal of the school is to provide opportunities for as many human beings as possible to achieve their highest potentials.

5. The school must provide an environment in which the individual can seek human values for himself or herself, with minimum damage to the freedom of choice and value assets of others.[93]

The aspects of the Lasswell value categories as adapted for education emphasize the need for the student to achieve a values balance in his or her life. In terms of self-analysis, each child must learn to analyze his or her value status in all eight value areas. A child that is over-indulged in power and deprived in affection is unbalanced. A child who has the respect of others but is deprived of skill is unbalanced.

This same principle of the balanced life must also be applied to the classroom, itself, where the classroom teacher has an important role in value-sharing with students. Besides acting as a questioner and clarifier of students' attitudes and values, the teacher can structure and manage classroom activities with the intent of achieving enhancement of each value category for students. In the section below, the role of the teacher and the classroom climate are described as they relate to the enhancement of each value area.

Value Category	*Role of the Teacher*
Affection	Provide a climate supporting acceptance, trust, emotional security, love, congeniality, friendship, and intimacy.
Respect	Provide an atmosphere in which each individual may achieve identity, a recognized social role, and self-esteem without fear of undeserved deprivation or penalties from others.
Skill	Provide opportunities for each student to develop his/her talents to the limits of his/her potential.
Enlightenment	Provide experiences for awareness and openness and encourage students to find their own truth in every issue without losing sight of their social norms and the significant events of human achievement.

Power	Provide situations in which the student will have opportunities to participate in making important decisions and to exert informal influence according to his/her talents and responsibilities.
Wealth	Provide facilities, materials, and services to promote excellent learning while guiding the student to produce wealth in the form of materials and services to himself/herself.
Well-being	Provide resource and interpersonal relationships which nurture the physical and mental health of each student.
Rectitude	Provide experiences enabling the student to develop a sense of responsibility for his/her own behavior, consideration for others, and a high sense of integrity.[94]

The American Institute for Character Education has designed the *Character Education Curriculum* to present students with selected concepts of character (or character traits).[95] Specifically, these standards of character and conduct involve being honest, generous, and just; living honorably; being kind and helpful to others; having convictions and courage; being tolerant; using one's time and talent creditably; providing security for one's self and dependents; fulfilling one's obligations as a citizen; standing for truth; and defending freedom's human rights.[96] These standards are abstracted from the "Freedom Code" as conceived by Russell Hill.[97]

The philosophy of the *Character Education Curriculum* is to provide a constructive and positive approach to develop strong, reliant character-based citizenship behaviors in children. The curriculum program attempts to enable students to understand themselves and determine their own attitudes, values, goals, objectives, ideals, and habits of life. Thomas Hopper, the President of the American Institute for Character Education, has stated, "Our aim is to help the child discover generally accepted values of our society and then allow him to choose those precepts that will direct his behavior. . . . the child who learns to consider all the available facts about the likely consequences of his behavior will choose to behave in ways satisfying to himself and to society."[98]

The *Character Education Curriculum* provides teachers with an opportunity to work with children on their mutual self-concepts, values clarification, and decision-making processes. The *Character Education Curriculum Teacher's Handbook*[99] advocates three teaching strategies for effective use of the materials. First, open-ended discussions are recommended. Here, the teacher's role in leading discussions is similar to the values clarification approach. Teachers are encouraged to respond to student's value statements with such questions as, "Why do you feel that way?"; "Do you think everyone should feel the same as you?"; "Can you understand why others might feel differently?"[100]

The process for decision-making is the second strategy identified. Teachers are to prepare children to make value judgments and decisions and consider alternatives and weigh outcomes. And thirdly, role-playing is recommended to strengthen the teaching of decision-making. In addition, story completion, art projects, posters, and sound filmstrips are all used to teach students.

The following lesson is from the Fifth Grade Teacher's Guide on the *Use of Time and Talents*.[101]

> Objective: At the conclusion of these lessons, your students should be able to identify the character traits that have contributed to the personal success of a well-known person.
>
> Step 1 • Ask the class this question: Is it important for only boys to try to use their time and talents creditably?
> • After a brief discussion, read the following story.

"WILMA"

When Wilma was just a baby, she was very small and frail for her age. She recovered from double pneumonia and scarlet fever, but lost the use of one leg due to nerve damage. If she ever expected to be able to walk, she needed to receive special treatments. Unfortunately, the clinic where treatment was available was 50 miles from her home. Although her mother worked six days a week, she took Wilma to the clinic on her day off over a period of two years. At night her brothers and sisters massaged her leg. Finally, the day came when Wilma was fitted for a shoe that allowed her to walk, but still with a limp.

At this time her older brother, who was anxious to help his younger sister, used his knowledge of basketball to interest Wilma in attempting some form of exercise. With a used fruit basket for a hoop and an old basketball, he taught her how to hold the ball and the best way to stand to get the ball into the basket.

Wilma became interested and began practicing. She never gave up. In 1960, the days of practicing, the hours of massage, the miles traveled to doctors, and, above all, the constant determination not to give up paid off for Wilma. The first

49

American woman to win *three* Olympic gold medals in track and to be named the number-one woman athlete of the year for both 1960 and 1961 was Wilma Rudolph.

Step II ● Ask for reactions to the story. Allow for a brief discussion. Ask the following questions:

1. From what has been read about Wilma Rudolph's life, can you name any other disadvantage she probably faced? (lack of money)
2. What were some of the reasons for her success?
3. Are all crippled and handicapped people able to overcome or change their lives the way Wilma Rudolph did?
4. Although her particular handicap could be overcome, would anyone blame her if she remained in bed for the rest of her life? Why?
5. Are people often inclined to give up rather than put forth the effort required to succeed?
6. Which of the traits we discussed in previous lessons were used by Wilma Rudolph?

SELECTED BIBLIOGRAPHY OF SUPPORTING CURRICULUM MATERIALS FOR VALUES INCULCATION

Arnspiger, Clyde; Brill, James; and Rucker, Ray W. *The Human Values Series* (grades K–6). Austin, Texas: Steck-Vaughn Co., 1967–1970.

Introduces stories to children within the Lasswell Value Framework of eight value categories:
Kindergarten: *The Human Values Series Teaching Pictures*, 1969.
First Grade: *Myself*, 1970.
Second Grade: *Myself and Others*, 1970.
Third Grade: *Our Values*, 1969.
Fourth Grade: *Values to Learn*, 1967.
Fifth Grade: *Values to Share*, 1967.
Sixth Grade: *Values to Live By*, 1967.

Bensley, Marvin L. *Coronado Plan for Preventive Drug Education: Teacher's Guides and Program Manuals.* San Diego, Calif.: Pennant, 1974.

This is a values-oriented approach to drug-abuse education. It focuses on developing decision-making skills, problem-solving skills, interpersonal relations, and clarifying values.

Brayer, Herbert O. *Teaching for Responsible Behavior:* "A Value-Oriented Approach to the Prevention of High Risk Behaviors Including Drug Abuse." Santa Ana, Calif.: Orange County Department of Education, 1975.

A curriculum guide for grades K–12 based upon the Lasswell Value Framework.

Brayer, Herbert O., and Cleary, Zella. *Valuing in the Family: A Workshop Guide*. San Diego, Calif.: Pennant Press, 1972.

Designed to help parents implement the Lasswell Value Framework in the home, encouraging respect and self-esteem in family relations.

The Character Education Curriculum. San Antonio, Texas: American Institute for Character Education, 1974. Grades 1–5.

Curriculum kit includes: teacher's guide, posters, activity sheets, and evaluation instruments.

Citizenship Decision-Making: Instructional Materials. Grades 4–6. (Citizenship Development Project, Richard C. Remy, director) Columbus (Mershon Center): Ohio State University, 1976.

The Lasswell Value Framework is used to teach citizenship education in the social studies.

Johnson, Spencer. *Value Tales*. San Diego, Calif.: Pennant Educational Materials. Attempts to inspire students by presenting examples of people who achieved good by good means. Students are taught by example to develop values. Grades K–6.

Louis Pasteur—*The Value of Believing in Yourself*
Helen Keller—*The Value of Determination*
The Wright Brothers—*The Value of Patience*
Elizabeth Fry—*The Value of Kindness*

Rucker, Ray; Arnspiger, C.; and Brodbeck, A. *Human Values in Education*. Dubuque, Iowa: Kendall/Hunt Publishing Co., 1969.

A basic text in the teaching of values. Introduces the Lasswell value categories for examining classroom experiences. Many teaching strategies and activities are provided.

Sayre, Joan. *Teaching Moral Values Through Behavior Modification*. Danville, Ill.: The Interstate, 1972.

Fifty-four page book containing 21 situation stories, including suggestions for guiding discussion of those stories, and an accompanying set of 84 picture cards designed to encourage students to think about and also accept certain moral values such as honesty, tolerance, sportsmanship, and responsibility. (Also in book form for intermediate grades.)

Simpson, Bert K. *Becoming Aware of Values*. San Diego, Calif.: Pennant Press, 1974.

Provides teaching to help students clarify their values, investigate goals, and develop decision-making skills. The Lasswell value categories are used as the basis for decision-making.

Teaching of Values: An Instructional Guide for Kindergarten, Grades 1–14. Los Angeles: Los Angeles City Schools, 1966.

Value Games which utilize the Lasswell value categories. Available from Pennant Educational Materials, San Diego, Calif.
1. *Balance in a Cruel, Cruel World* (grade 6–adult)
2. *Helping Hands* (grade K–3)
3. *Match Wits* (grade 6–adult)
4. *My Cup Runneth Over* (grade 6–adult)
5. *Timao* (grade 6–adult)
6. *Value Bingo* (grade 4–adult)

Value Measures which utilize the Lasswell value categories. Available from Pennant Educational Materials, San Diego, Calif.
1. *Gardner Analysis of Personality Survey.* Lawrence E. Gardner, 1972.
2. *Me and You Inventory.* Lida C. Colwell, Louise B. Taylor, and Bert K. Simpson. Grades K–1 level and Grades 2–3 level.
3. *The Murphy Inventory of Values.* Maribeth L. Murphy, 1969.
4. *Perception of Values Inventory Manual; A Combined Sociometric/Personality Approach for Fourth Grade Through Adult.* Bert K. Simpson, 1973.
5. *Risk-Taking Attitudes Values Inventory.* Richard E. Carney. Five levels: primary, elementary, secondary, post-high school, and mature adult. Useful for drug, alcohol abuse, family life, and mental health programs.
6. *Values Inventory of Behavioral Responses Manual, Grades 4, 5, and 6.* Nancy Seiders and Edward Sanford, 1971.

Moral Reasoning and Cognitive Moral Development

The cognitive moral-reasoning approach to values education is based upon the theory and research of cognitive moral development by Lawrence Kohlberg. As described previously, Kohlberg presents a developmental view of morality and identifies three levels and six stages of development. The central concern of this approach is the reasoning and kinds of motives a child uses to justify a moral choice.

Kohlberg has defined the aim of moral education as "the stimulation of the next step of development,"[102] and he has found that this occurs naturally when children are given opportunities to exercise their capacity for moral judgment. The highest stages of reasoning involve the ability and disposition to make value judgments on the basis of universal principles of justice; that is, "universal modes of choosing which we wish all men to apply to all situations and which represent morally self-justifying reasons for action."[103]

Kohlberg's approach to values education aims at developing the student's ability to understand situations of moral conflict and to develop more complex moral reasoning through successive and sequential stages. A main tenet of cognitive moral reasoning is that children are attracted to higher levels of reasoning.[104] When a child is presented with arguments both for and against a course of action in a moral dilemma, the effect depends on the level of the argument. Although children at higher stages influence the reasoning of those at lower stages, the reverse is not true. Research findings indicate that children will reject judgments below their own level as inadequate ways of thinking, but will understand and prefer judgments made from the point of view of one level of development higher than their own.

Kohlberg has identified several conditions which appear to be important in conducting moral education.[105] These conditions which focus on classroom discussion are drawn from research that indicates moral discussions can result in upward stage movement of moral reasoning. They are:

1. Knowledge of the child's stage of functioning. (Understanding the meaning of the moral judgments made by the child.)

2. Exposing the child to reasoning one stage above the child's own thoughts.

3. Exposing children to problematic situations which pose genuine moral conflict and disagreement. (Posing problems and contradictions for the child's current moral structure will lead the child to be dissatisfied with his/her current level.)

4. Creating an atmosphere of interchange and dialogue in which conflicting moral views are compared in an open manner. (The teacher's task here is to help the child see inconsistencies and inadequacies in his/her way of thinking and finding ways to resolve such inconsistencies and inadequacies.)

One widely used method to stimulate the development of more mature moral reasoning has been the discussion of moral issues in the form of dilemmas. Moral dilemmas are those situations in which values conflict—where claims can be made for several choices and where each choice is made at the price of another. Students are asked to think about how the dilemmas should be resolved, to identify the moral issues involved, and to offer reasons justifying their positions.

During the discussion, the teacher encourages students to comment on and challenge each other's reasoning. The main focus of dilemma discussion is on the students' reasoning rather than the particular choices they make on a dilemma. The complexity and range of the content of dilemmas depend upon the maturity and ability of the students.

A good moral dilemma has five general characteristics:[106]

1. It builds upon the work in the course. (Dilemmas may be derived from real-life situations in contemporary society, life experiences of students, or course-related content.)

2. It should be as simple as possible, having a central character or primary group of characters.

3. It should be open-ended. (There should be no single, obvious, or culturally approved right answer.)

4. It should involve two or more issues that have moral implications.

5. It should offer a choice of actions and pose the question, "What *should* the central character do?" (This should help students to engage in moral reasoning about the conflict presented in the dilemma.)

Dilemmas can be presented in a variety of ways: in writing or orally; through a film, recording, or sound-filmstrip; through a role-playing exercise, simulation game, or skit; or by way of a story or historical document.

The dilemma presented below is intended for junior and senior high school students. It was written at the Social Studies Curriculum Center at Carnegie-Mellon University.[107]

"SHARON'S DILEMMA"

Sharon and Jill were best friends. One day they went shopping together. Jill tried on a sweater and then, to Sharon's surprise, walked out of the store wearing the sweater under her coat. A moment later, the store's security officer stopped Sharon and demanded that she tell him the name of the girl who had walked out. He told the storeowner that he had seen the two girls together, and that he was sure that the one who left had been shoplifting. The storeowner told Sharon that she could really get in trouble if she didn't give her friend's name.

Should Sharon tell? Why?

While working with the Carnegie-Mellon/Harvard Values Education Project, T. M. Jones and R. E. Galbraith created an instructional model for teaching a moral dilemma (see Figure 2).[108] This model is expanded in their book, *Moral Reasoning: A Teaching Handbook for Adapting Kohlberg to the Classroom*.[109] Jones and Galbraith have identified four steps for leading a discussion of a moral dilemma:

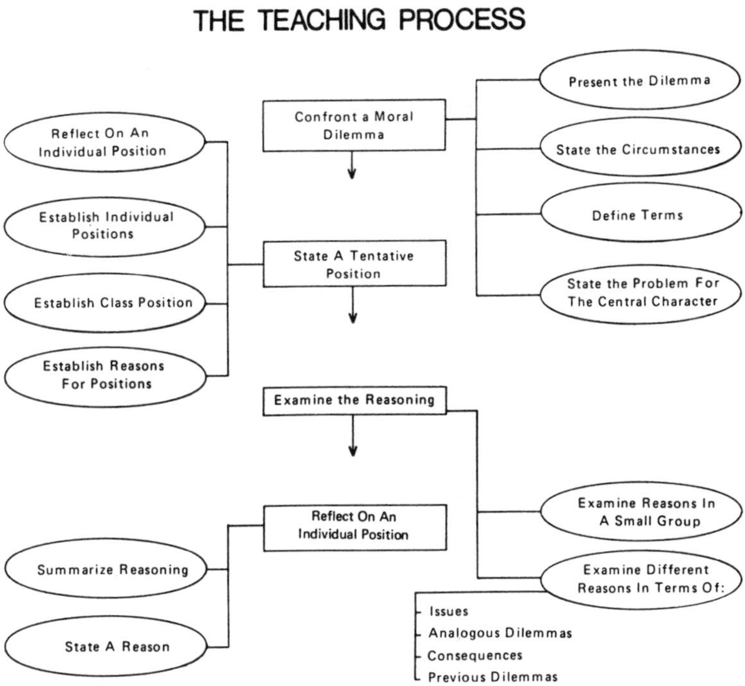

THE TEACHING PROCESS

FIG. 2—Diagram of the teaching process for teaching a moral dilemma, from *Moral Reasoning: Teaching Strategies for Adapting Kohlberg to the Classroom*, by Ronald E. Galbraith and Thomas M. Jones, p. 64. Greenhaven Press, Inc., 1611 Polk St., N.E., Minneapolis, MN 55413.

1. Confronting a moral dilemma

2. Having students state a tentative position on the dilemma

3. Examining or "testing" the student's reasoning for a position on the dilemma

4. Having students summarize reasons and reflect on an individual position in resolving the dilemma.

The most important step in the process is examining the reasoning. During this time, the students have an opportunity to test their reasoning against the thinking of others, and the teacher can raise questions to clarify the moral issues, raise analogous dilemmas, and structure role-playing. In the final step, the purpose is not to reach a classroom consensus, but rather to engage each individual student in thinking about the best response to a difficult moral problem.

Several other techniques have been suggested for leading moral discussions in classrooms.[110] The leader should--

1. Establish a supportive, non-judgmental atmosphere. (It is important to recognize the student's right to hold and express views without sanctioning those views as right or justifiable.)

2. Seat students so that they can see and hear each other.

3. Listen carefully to what students say.

4. Ask questions which do not threaten students.

5. Encourage student-to-student interaction.

6. Develop discussion skills in students.

7. Keep the class working constructively by using probe questions, alternative dilemmas, or dilemmas which have been used previously in the course.

8. Plan carefully but remain flexible to cope with substantive diversions.

9. Get someone to tape your class.

10. Relax and enjoy it.

Besides the discussion of moral dilemmas, some additional teaching activities for stimulating moral development are suggested by Frank Simon,[111] Robert P. Craig,[112] Lawrence Kohlberg,[113] and Clive Beck.[114] Simon says that the elementary teacher who teaches children at the pre-conventional level should employ motivational appeals and teaching-learning activities which appeal to and develop the child's desire for social approval and acceptance. He suggests that children be rewarded (non-materially) for behavior which indicates assuming responsibility, working well with others, and respecting the rights of others. The use of punishment should be discouraged since it appeals to the lowest stage of development.

Craig urges teachers at any level to allow students as much freedom as possible in making decisions. To enable students in developing a sense of justice and reciprocity, he advocates that students should help decide classroom procedures and rules. Here, it is important that students recognize the distinction between procedural rules and moral rules. Finally, Craig claims that there needs to be a general consistency in the administration of school and classroom rules.

Kohlberg also encourages students' participation in classroom decisions. He encourages elementary teachers to foster interaction and develop patterns of cooperation among children. Kohlberg argues for the creation of a moral classroom atmosphere and a just classroom environment.

Beck advocates the creation of mini-courses in values that could be inserted in the school curriculum. "They could be studied as wholes or in fragments."[115] He also proposes a coordinated, interdepartmental program in values. Among the subject areas in which the study of values might occur are family living, social studies, and guidance at the elementary level, and health, physical education, history, people and society, English, guidance, and home economics at the secondary level. R. L. Mosher and N. A. Sprinthall[116] have described a successful guidance program focusing on moral development entitled "Deliberate Psychological Education."

BACKGROUND READING FOR TEACHING MORAL REASONING AND MORAL DEVELOPMENT

Beck, Clive M. *Moral Education in the Schools: Some Practical Suggestions. Profiles in Practical Education.* Toronto: (Ontario Institute for Studies in Education) OISE Publications, 1971. No. 3.

Beyer, Barry K. "Conducting Moral Discussions in the Classroom." *Social Education.* Vol. 40, No. 4, April 1976, pp. 194–202.

Blatt, Moshe, and Kohlberg, Lawrence. "The Effects of Classroom Moral Discussion Upon Children's Level of Moral Judgment." *Journal of Moral Education.* Vol. 4, February 1975, pp. 129–162.

Catalogue of Teaching and Research Materials in Moral Education. Vancouver, British Columbia: Association for Values Education and Research, 1975.

Crittenden, Brian. *Form and Content in Moral Education.* Monograph Series #2. Toronto: Ontario Institute for Studies in Education, 1972.

Duska, Ronald, and Whelan, Mariellen. *Moral Development: A Guide to Piaget and Kohlberg.* New York: Paulist Press, 1975.

Fenton, Edwin; Colby, Ann; and Speicher-Dubin, Betsy. "Developing Moral Dilemmas for Social Studies Classes." Unpublished paper from Moral Education and Research Foundation, Harvard University, 1974.

Galbraith, Ronald E., and Jones, Thomas M. *Moral Reasoning: Teaching Strategies for Adapting Kohlberg to the Classroom.* Anoka, Minn.: Greenhaven Press, Inc., 1976.

_____. "Teaching Strategies for Moral Dilemmas." *Social Education.* Vol. 39, No. 1, January 1975, pp. 16–22.

_____. "Teaching Strategies for Moral Dilemmas: An Application of Kohlberg's Theory of Moral Development to the Social Studies Classroom." *Social Studies Journal.* Vol. III, No. I, Spring 1974.

Hall, Robert T., and Davis, John U. *Moral Education in Theory and Practice.* Buffalo, N.Y.: Prometheus Books, 1975.

Kohlberg, Lawrence. "The Child as a Moral Philosopher." *Psychology Today.* Vol. 7, September 1968, pp. 25–30.

_____. "The Cognitive-Developmental Approach to Moral Education." *Phi Delta Kappan.* Vol. LVI, No. 10, June 1975, pp. 670–677.

_____. "Moral Development and the New Social Studies." *Social Education.* Vol. 37, No. 5, May 1973, pp. 369–375.

_____. "Moral Education for a Society in Moral Transition." *Educational Leadership.* October 1975, pp. 46–54.

Kohlberg, Lawrence, and Turiel, Elliot. "Moral Development and Moral Education." *Psychology and Educational Practice.* (Edited by Gerald Lesser.) Glenview, Ill.: Scott, Foresman, & Co., 1971.

Kohlberg, Lawrence, with Whitten, Phillip. "Understanding the Hidden Curriculum." *Learning.* Vol. 1, No. 2, 1972, pp. 10–14.

Mattox, Beverly A. *Getting it Together: Dilemmas for the Classroom Based on Kohlberg's Approach.* San Diego: Pennant Press, 1975.

Mosher, Ralph L., and Sullivan, Paul R. "A Curriculum in Moral Education for Adolescents." *Journal of Moral Education.* Vol. 5, No. 2, pp. 159–172.

_____. "Moral Education: A New Initiative for Guidance." *Focus on Guidance.* Vol. 6, No. 5, 1974, pp. 1–12.

Pagliuso, Susan. *A Workbook: Understanding Stages of Development.* Toronto, Ontario: Ontario Institute for Studies in Education, 1975.

Porter, Nancy, and Taylor, Nancy. *A Handbook for Assessing Moral Reasoning.* Toronto, Ontario: Ontario Institute for Studies in Education, 1972.

Rest, Jim. "Developmental Psychology as a Guide to Value Education: A Review of Kohlbergian Programs." *Review of Educational Research.* Vol. 44, Spring 1974, pp. 241–258.

Selman, Robert L., and Lieberman, Marcus. "Moral Education in the Primary Grades: An Evaluation of a Developmental Curriculum." *Journal of Educational Psychology.* Vol. 67, No. 5, October 1975, pp. 712–716.

Simon, Frank. "Moral Development: Some Suggested Implications for Teaching." *Journal of Moral Education.* Vol. 5, No. 2, pp. 173–178.

Sullivan, Edmund V. *Moral Learning: Findings, Issues, and Questions.* New York: Paulist Press, 1975.

Wilson, John. *Ideals: A Guide to Moral and Metaphysical Outlooks.* New York: Morehouse Barlow Co., 1974.

_____. *A Teacher's Guide to Moral Education.* London: Geoffrey Chapman, 1973.

_____. *Practical Methods of Moral Education.* London: Heinemann, 1972.

Wilson, John; Williams, Norman; and Sugarman, Barry. *Introduction to Moral Education.* London: Penguin Books, 1967.

SELECTED BIBLIOGRAPHY OF SUPPORTING CURRICULUM MATERIALS FOR MORAL DEVELOPMENT

Altshuler, Thelma. *Choices: Situations to Stimulate Thought and Expression.* Englewood Cliffs, N.J.: Prentice-Hall, 1970.

This source provides a variety of potential dilemma situations which might be adapted for use in a high school or junior college classroom.

Blatt, Moshe; Colby, Ann; and Speicher-Dubin, Betsy. *Hypothetical Dilemmas for Use in Moral Discussions.* Cambridge, Mass.: Center for Moral Development and Moral Education, Harvard University, 1974.

Handbook of varied moral dilemmas appropriate for use with adolescents and adults. Includes questions for stimulating discussion and probing the reasoning of students.

Decades of Decisions. National Geographic Film Series on Public Broadcasting System.

Dramatizes the moral dilemmas faced by early Americans at the time of the new nation.

"Deciding Right from Wrong: The Dilemma of Morality Today." White Plains, N.Y.: Center for Humanities.

A two-set Carousel slide-tape program which focuses on the judgment-making process. "Through consideration of contemporary, historical and literary examples, students are encouraged to examine the origins of their own and society's standards of right and wrong. Investigates the role of conscience in facing personal dilemmas and deals with public morality and the high cost of upholding principles."

Exploring Value Dilemmas and Decisions: Alternatives, Criteria and Consequences. Produced by XICOM Inc., 1972, distributed by NTL Learning Resources Corp., Fairfax, Va.

Four packages of filmstrips-tapes present core value dilemmas from youth to adults.

Fenton, Edwin, general editor. *Holt Social Studies Curriculum—2nd Edition.* N.Y.: Holt, Rinehart, & Winston, 1974.

Incorporates valuing questions and dilemmas to encourage moral development. Each volume and each teacher's guide includes a series of dilemma stories which fit into the curriculum. Dilemmas appear on ditto masters in the audiovisual kit.

Fenton, Edwin, and Kohlberg, Lawrence. *Learning to Lead Moral Discussions: A Teacher Preparation Kit.* Pleasantville, N.Y.: Guidance Associates, Fall 1976.

––––––––––. *Moral Issues in American History.* Pleasantville, N.Y.: Guidance Associates, Fall 1976. Filmstrip.

––––––––––. *Moral Issues in Civics/Problem of Democracy.* Pleasantville, N.Y.: Guidance Associates, available Fall 1976. Filmstrip.

Galbraith, Ronald E., and Jones, Thomas M. *Moral Reasoning: Teaching Strategies for Adapting Kohlberg to the Classroom.* Anoka, Minn.: Greenhaven Press, Inc., 1976.

Explains the teaching process for classroom implementation of moral reasoning and development based on the theory of Lawrence Kohlberg. Illustrates how to have students confront a moral problem, take a moral stand, develop supporting reasons, and test their reasoning through group discussions. Presents sample dilemmas and provides instructions for creating dilemmas in your own classroom.

Grainger, A. J. *The Bullring: A Classroom Experiment in Moral Education.* London: Pergamon Press, 1970.

Presents a teacher's attempt to introduce moral education in a high school setting. Many activities are described.

Hall, Brian. *The Development of Consciousness: A Confluent Theory of Values.* New York: Paulist Press, 1975.

Offers a synthesis of moral development, values clarification, and cognitive learning.

"How Moral Am I?" *The Development of Moral Behavior: A Multimedia Exploration for Parents, Teachers, and Students.* New York: W. H. Sadlier Inc., 1973.

A two-part filmstrip-record set which explains Kohlberg's stage theory. With teacher's guide.

Human Values Series: Value Films. Middletown, Conn.: Xerox Education Publications, 1975. Elementary, intermediate, and secondary level cartoon fables.

Kohlberg, Lawrence, and Selman, Robert. *First Things: Values.* New York: Guidance Associates, 1972.

Each sound filmstrip unit presents two open-ended moral dilemmas. Each set also includes a teacher's guide which briefly discusses the theory and how to work with children in a discussion format. Instructional filmstrip also available.

Levin, Malcolm A., and Eisenberg, John A. *Dilemma.* Toronto: Holt, Rinehart, & Winston of Canada, Limited, 1971.

A series of stories (pamphlets) designed to provide dilemmas for students to discuss many social problems.

Lickona, Thomas. *A Strategy for Teaching Values.* New York: Guidance Associates, 1971.

An in-service training component to accompany *First Things: Values Series.* Three sound filmstrips and discussion guide present theoretical background, examples of implementation, and a model lesson.

Lifeline (Values Education Curriculum, Peter McPhail, director). Niles, Ill.: Argus Communications, 1975.

These curriculum materials were produced by the Schools Council Moral Education Curriculum Project, based at the Oxford University Dept. of Education. The material (cards, booklets, and books) has been designed to encourage moral and social development in upper elementary and junior high school students. The teacher's book, *Learning to Care*, gives a full background to the project's research and provides suggestions for classroom use.

Lockwood, Alan. *Moral Reasoning: The Value of Life.* XEP Public Issues Series. Middletown, Conn.: Xerox Education Publication, 1972.

A booklet prepared as part of the Harvard Social Studies Project series. The booklet is especially interesting for integrating Kohlberg materials with the format developed by Oliver and Newmann. An extended presentation of actual documented cases is used to set up discussions (for instance, a discussion of Bonhoeffer's complicity in the plot to kill Hitler; Calley and My Lai, etc.).

Mackey, James A. "Discussing Moral Dilemmas in the Classroom." *English Journal.* December 1975, pp. 28–30.

Presents sample moral dilemmas.

————. "Moral Insight in the Classroom." *Elementary School Journal.* February 1973.

Presents sample moral dilemmas.

Mattox, Beverly A. *Getting it Together: Dilemmas for the Classroom Based on Kohlberg's Approach.* San Diego: Pennant Press, 1975.

Presents many value dilemmas applicable from first grade to high school and discusses ways of using moral education in the classroom.

"Moral Decision Making." Los Angeles, Calif.: Oxford Films, Inc.

A series of five short films which provide open-ended moral dilemmas. For elementary and junior high students. Study guide is included with each film. Titles are:
"Aggression-Assertion"
"Cheating"
"Sharing"
"Response to Misbehavior"
"Stealing."

Personal Feelings of Responsibility. Troy, Mich.: Education Corporation of America.

Seven sound filmstrips concerning different areas of ethical behavior.

Photo Study Cards and Discussion Kits. Anoka, Minn.: Greenhaven Press, Inc.

Each picture card presents students with moral dilemmas and discussion activities on meaning and values. For each dilemma, six responses are provided as possible alternatives to the moral problem under consideration. Each of the six responses represents a different stage in Kohlberg's six stages of moral reasoning. 1. Who Are You? 2. Who Would You Like to Be? 3. What Do You Value? 4. You and Authority 5. You and Social Responsibility.

Raths, L. E. *Exploring Moral Values: An Introduction for Students.* Pleasantville, N.Y.: Warren Schloat Production, 1969.

One record, 15 filmstrips presenting 44 critical open-ended dilemmas. Topics include prejudice, honesty, authority, and personal values.

Rifley, Jean. *Tackle Values and Feelings.* Minneapolis, Minn.: T. S. Denison and Co. Inc.

Activity cards present problem situations and moral dilemmas in a format designed for individuals, small groups, or class use.

Rules. Boulder, Colo.: Biological Science Curriculum Study, 1974.

One of the modules in the Human Sciences Program for grades 4–7. This module is grouped into three problem areas: "Is There A Rule?", "What Should I Do?", and "How Do Rules Change?" A large-scale simulation game is included as an integrative activity. Many of these activities are specifically designed to stimulate moral reasoning.

Searching for Values: A Film Anthology. New York: Learning Corporation of America, 1972.

15 film series for high school made up from edited feature motion pictures. Each film presents a dramatic situation centering around a theme which involves a specific question, moral dilemma, or decision. Teacher's manual is supplied.

Selman, Robert. "First Things: Social Reasoning." New York: Guidance Associates, 1975.

Based on Selman's work on role-taking, these sound filmstrips present problems designed for discussion among elementary school children that will foster social and moral development. Titles are:
"How Do You Know What Others Will Do?"
"How Would You Feel . . . ?"
"How Do You Know What's Fair?"
"How Can You Work Things Out?"
Instructional filmstrip also available.

Selman, Robert, and Kohlberg, Lawrence. *Psychological Moral Dilemmas for Adolescents.* Pleasantville, N.Y.: Guidance Associates, Fall 1976.

Six American Families. Based on Paul Wilke's book, *Trying Out the Dream.*

This is a series of television programs which present moral dilemmas to viewers. The series shows "real" situations about how people live, how they make decisions, and how they relate to each other. (Westinghouse Stations)

A Strategy for Teaching Social Reasoning. New York: Guidance Associates.

An in-service unit presents the theory of social reasoning, describes children's social reasoning behavior and demonstrates classroom implementation of *First Things: Social Reasoning.* Two sound filmstrips and teacher's guide.

Unfinished Stories. Garden City, N.Y.: Doubleday and Co., Inc.

A series of short films primarily designed for junior high school students. Each film portrays a conflict of conscience and then leaves it up to the students to decide what they should do.

Unfinished Stories and More Unfinished Stories. Washington, D.C.: NEA.

For elementary through middle grade students. Open-ended situations which can be used for values clarification and moral discussions.

Values. Jamaica, N.Y.: Eyegate House.

Six sound filmstrips designed to explore areas of value development. Titles are: "Telling the Truth," "What is Stealing," "Kindness," "Politeness," "Responsibility," "Citizenship."

Value Filmstrips. Middletown, Conn.: Xerox Education Publications, 1975.

Seven cartoon filmstrips which present fables on questions such as: What are the measures of success and happiness? How important is self-discipline? Must things always be the way they are? Elementary level.

The Watergate Curriculum: Ethics and Morality in Government. Washington, D.C.: NEA.

A three-unit program on values and contemporary morality as symbolized in Watergate. Each unit contains a printed copy of the student book plus a set of duplicating masters. Titles are: "What Is Playing For" (K–4), "Learning to Govern" (5–8), "The Individual, The Constitution, and Watergate" (9–14).

Wills, Larry Dean, and Skaggs, David Curtis. "Using Moral Dilemmas to Study the American Revolution." *Social Education.* May, 1976, Vol. 40, No. 5, pp. 307–309.

Presents moral dilemmas for teaching the American Revolution.

Values Analysis

Values analysis is mainly a cognitive and rational approach to understanding values. Values analysis is derived from the scientific method and provides a systematic, logical approach to value reasoning and resolving value conflicts. "Students are urged to provide verifiable facts about the goodness or worth of phenomena. Valuing is the cognitive process of determining and justifying these facts."[117]

Values analysis is usually applied to work out positions on public policy or social value issues. Although this approach does not focus explicitly on moral issues, moral statements are presumed to be factual statements, and thus, subject to empirical study.[118]

The objectives of value analysis are described by Jerrold R. Coombs in *Values Education: Rationale, Strategies, and Procedures:*[119]

1. Teaching students to rate a value object in a particular way.

2. Helping students to make the most rational judgment they can make about the value object in question.

3. Teaching students to make rational value judgments.

4. Teaching students how to operate as members of a group attempting to come to a common value judgment about some value object.

Coombs also specifies the standards of or conditions which a value judgment must meet to qualify as rational or defensible:[120]

1. The purported facts supporting the judgment must be true or well confirmed.

2. The facts must be genuinely relevant, i.e., they must actually have valence for the person making the judgment.

3. Other things being equal, the greater the range of relevant facts taken into account in making the judgment, the more adequate the judgment is likely to be.

4. The value principle implied by the judgment must be acceptable to the person making the judgment.

There is no single sanctioned strategy to teach values analysis. Rather there are several prominent models which have been frequently used in social studies education. Most notable are models proposed by J. R. Coombs and M. Meux in the 41st National Council for the Social Studies Yearbook, *Values Education: Rationale, Strategies, and Procedures,*[121] Donald Oliver, James P. Shaver, and Fred M. Newmann,[122] Byron G. Massialas and C. Benjamin Cox,[123] M. P. Hunt and L. E. Metcalf,[124] and Jack R. Fraenkel.[125] Although each model proposed by the above educators differs from the other, each emphasizes the rational analysis of value statements and judgments as well as the resolution of value conflicts. Students are asked to follow specific steps in their analysis of public or social issues.

The teaching methods most frequently used in the analysis approach to values education are individual and group study of problems and issues, library and field research, and rational, Socratic class discussions.[126] Coombs and Meux specify three teaching strategies which enhance the outcomes of value analysis:[127]

1. The teacher should *actively* engage the student in the operations required to carry out each of the six tasks described above. As the student's familiarity with these operations increases, he/she should be given increased responsibility for initiating them and carrying them out on his/her own.

2. The teacher should point out what task is to be accomplished by each of the operations in which the teacher engages students.

3. The teacher should point out the importance of each of these tasks in terms of meeting the standards of rational evaluation.

The analytical process proposed by Coombs and Meux identifies the following tasks:

1. Identifying and clarifying the value question by defining terms and providing examples.

2. Assembling (gathering and organizing) purported facts (facts relevant to answer the value question).

3. Assessing the truth of purported facts.

4. Clarifying the relevance of the facts to value questions.

5. Arriving at a tentative value decision.

6. Testing the value principle implied in the decision (determining whether or not the decision is acceptable).[128]

JURISPRUDENTIAL MODEL

Oliver, Shaver, and Newmann have structured a policy-making and valuing strategy whereby public controversy can be resolved through rational discussion.[129] Their project accepts the dignity and worth of the individual as a high level, given value. But rather than deducing a specific moral code from this general value, they believe that in the process of justifying a particular kind of social conduct, one might appeal to this ultimate value.

Newmann suggests that public policy issues involve three components: (1) a moral-value issue, (2) a definitional issue, and (3) a fact-explanation issue.[130] He discusses several strategies for clarifying value statements. They are valid only if it is assumed that the discussants are committed to "American creed," such values as "justice," "equality," and "human dignity." Strategies which can resolve value issues include: illuminating the relationship between specific and higher order values, determining value conflicts resulting from inconsistencies in personal positions, and dealing with incompatible frameworks.

Oliver and Shaver place the operations of clarifying public controversy in the following order:

1. Abstracting general values from concrete situations

2. Using general value concepts as dimensional constructs

3. Identifying conflicts between value constructs

4. Identifying a class of value conflict situations

5. Discovering or creating value conflict situations which are analagous to the problem under consideration

6. Working toward a general qualified position

7. Testing the factual assumptions behind a qualified value position

8. Testing the relevance of statements.[131]

ADJUDICATING JUDGMENTS-OF-VALUE MODEL

The model developed by Massialas and Cox[132] assumes that values can be assessed and social issues resolved only when a dissenting group can identify a root value on which consensus can be reached. When a group has reached agreement on a high-level value, the values in conflict can be considered in terms of whether they lead to consequences consistent with the higher level value. Once a third or higher level is agreed upon by the group, the scientific method of inquiry can be used to determine which course of action or instrumental value will most likely result in the realization of the higher value accepted by all members of the group.

Massialas and Cox have summarized their decision-making model by using an example:

ADJUDICATING JUDGMENTS OF VALUE

1. What value judgment is made regarding the occupation of persons in the United States?

Given value judgment:
White persons, particularly white Christians, should be given the more skilled jobs, the positions of executive authority in most businesses, high governmental offices, and professional positions.

2. What *opposing* value judgment is also made by many persons in the United States which is clearly contradictory to the value judgment *given* above?

3. If the *given* judgment were acted upon in the United States, what consequences are predicted in terms of the practices and policies which would be put into effect? What factual consequences would be expected to result if the *given* value judgment were acted upon?

4. Can you offer any *proof* that any of the above predictions for the *given* value judgment would actually take place?

5. If the *opposing* value judgment were acted upon in the United States, what consequences are predicted in terms of the practices and policies which would be put into effect? What factual consequences would be expected to result if the *opposing* value judgment were acted upon?

6. Can you offer any proof that any of the above predictions for the *opposing* value judgment would actually take place?

7. What *third* value would you propose as being relatively noncontroversial and logically appropriate to use for judging between the *given* and *opposing* values?

8. Which of the value judgments, the *given* or *opposing*, appears to be more clearly instrumental in achieving the *third*, relatively noncontroversial value?

9. In a concise statement support your choice of either the *given* or *opposing* value by giving the reasons for choosing the one and for rejecting the other.

10. In summary, assuming you have proved your case, state the relationship between the *given* or *opposing* value judgment and the *third*, noncontroversial value in the following formula:
"If either the *given* value judgment OR the *opposing* value judgment—NOT BOTH, then (the *third*, noncontroversial value) will be achieved."[133]

PROJECTING CONSEQUENCES MODEL

Hunt and Metcalf have devised a teaching model for the clarification of values and the making of policy decisions.[134] This model emphasizes the analysis of value concepts and the consideration of the consequences of value alternatives. Using this model, the students define value concepts, project consequences, appraise them using set criteria, and attempt to justify the criteria used to evaluate the consequences. A summary of their model is presented below:

I. What is the nature of the object, event, or policy to be evaluated? This question plainly poses a task in concept analysis. If the students are trying to evaluate the welfare state, they should define this object as precisely and clearly as possible.
   A. How is the welfare state to be defined intentionally and extensively? By what criteria is it to be defined intensionally?
   B. If students disagree over criteria, and therefore in their definition of welfare state, how is this disagreement to be treated? Must they agree? Can they agree to disagree? Are there criteria by which welfare state ought to be defined? On what basis can we select among different sets of criteria?

II. The consequences problem.
   A. What consequences can be expected or anticipated from the policy in question. Is it true, as some have claimed, that the growth of the welfare state destroys individual incentive? How does one get evidence for answering this kind of question?
   B. If students disagree in their projection of consequences, how is this difference to be treated? Can evidence produce agreement? What is the difference between a disagreement over *criteria* and a disagreement over *evidence?*

III. Appraisal of consequences.
   A. Are the projected consequences desirable or not?
   B. By what criteria are the consequences to be appraised? How do different criteria affect one's appraisal of consequences?

IV. Justification of criteria.
   A. Can criteria for appraising consequences be justified? How?
   B. If students disagree on criteria, and therefore in their appraisal of consequences, how can this difference be treated? What relationship ought to exist between one's criteria and one's basic philosophy of life?
   C. Are students consistent in their use of criteria?[135]

ANALYSIS OF VALUE INCIDENTS MODEL

Jack Fraenkel has developed several strategies based upon the presentation of "value incidents" to identify values and explore human conflicts.[136] "A value incident is a situation, statement, argument, excerpt from a play or novel, picture, cartoon or the like, in which one or more individuals say or do something that he, she or they indicate (or imply) is important to them."[137] The students are asked to make inferences about what the character in the value incident considers to be important and to hypothesize what they would do in the situation.

Students begin to identify and analyze values by responding to the following set of questions:

1. What did the key people do or say in the situation just presented?

2. What do you think were their reasons for doing/saying what they did?

3. What do these reasons you've identified tell you about what is important to these people?

4. If you were in a situation like this, what would you do?

5. Why would you do this?

6. What differences do you see in what all these people think is important? Similarities? How would you explain such differences/similarities?[138]

Open-ended value incidents can also be used to explore value conflicts. For this strategy, the characters in the value incident should be facing a choice between two or conflicting alternatives. Students give responses to the following questions:

1. What is the story about?

2. What options are open to the key persons involved?

3. What might happen to them if they do each of these things (i.e., what might be the consequences of the various options)?

4. What might happen to those who are immediately involved? What evidence, if any, is there that these consequences will indeed occur?

5. What do you think they should do? Why?

6. Has anything like this ever happened to you?

7. What did you do?

8. As you think back now, was that a good or bad thing to do? Why?

9. What else could you have done?[139]

The teacher's role in Fraenkel's model is to assist students in evaluating the various value statements and "value claims," and to help students learn to evaluate alternatives, consequences, and conclusions by searching for evidence. Fraenkel explains the intent of this strategy as follows:

> Underlying this strategy is the assumption that through realizing, discussing, and evaluating various courses of action—along with the consequences of these options and the evidence to support or refute these consequences—students will become more aware that all of us hold values that will conflict at times, realize that there are many different ways of dealing with a particular problem, and, hopefully, become more willing to think about and evaluate the consequences which various options may produce.[140]

SELECTED BIBLIOGRAPHY OF SUPPORTING CURRICULUM MATERIALS FOR VALUES ANALYSIS

Bauer, Nancy W. "Value Seeking in the Classroom," *Teacher's Notebook.* New York: School Department of Harcourt, Brace Jovanovich, 1970.

An essay which describes how values analysis can be used to resolve social issues.

Bender, David L., and McCuen, Gary E., editors. *Opposing Viewpoints Series.* Minneapolis, Minn.: Greenhaven Press, Inc., 1971–1974.

Title: *American Values*—collection of readings holding on a variety of positions on such topics as values in business, politics, society, religion, and patriotism.

Berlak, Harold, and Tomlinson, Timothy R. *People/Choices/Decisions.* New York: Random House, 1973.

Titles are: A Village Family
One City Neighborhood
Changing Neighborhoods

Units have been designed to involve children in examining social and ethical issues emphasizing skills in analyzing and clarifying values and resolving value conflicts.

Brandwein, Paul F. *The Social Sciences/Concepts and Values. Sources of Identity-Settings for Change.* New York: Harcourt Brace Jovanovich, 1972.

71

The twelve units of this interdisciplinary curriculum are structured so that students are asked to make decisions that reflect on values on the basis of evidence and personal experience.

Brandwein, Paul F., editor. *The Social Sciences/Concepts and Values.* New York: Harcourt, Brace Jovanovich, 1970.

Elementary social science series designed to enable students to analyze human behavior and human values.

Durkin, Mary C., and McNaughton, Anthony H. *The Taba Program in Social Science.* Menlo Park, Calif.: Addison Wesley, 1972–1974.

A major aspect of TABA is its focus on the examination of feelings, attitudes, and values.

Farren, F. J., and Mesmer, A. W. *It's Your Decision.* Vestal, N.Y.: Values Perspectives Associates, 1975.

Values analysis is used to help students confront, analyze, and resolve dilemmas. Sample dilemmas are included.

Fraenkel, Jack R. "Strategies for Developing Values," *Today's Education.* Vol. 63, No. 7, Nov.–Dec. 1973, pp. 49–55.

Presents teaching strategies for identifying values and value conflicts through the use of value incidents.

————————. "Value Education in the Social Studies," *Phi Delta Kappan.* Vol. 50, No. 8, April, 1969, pp. 457–461.

A discussion of values analysis. Appropriate teaching strategies are provided.

Gray, Charles E. "Value Inquiry and the Social Studies," *Education.* Vol. 93, No. 2, pp. 130–137.

Presents an overview of teaching strategies enabling students to analyze and compare value systems and to analyze and test value judgments.

Hunt, Maurice P., and Metcalf, Lawrence E. *Teaching High School Social Studies.* New York: Harper and Row, 1968.

A teaching model for the clarification and analysis of values in the making of public policy decisions.

Lippitt, Ronald; Fox, Robert; and Schaible, Lucille. *Social Science Laboratory Units.* Chicago, Ill.: Science Research Associates, Inc.

An intermediate grade curriculum providing a modified laboratory approach into the causes and effects of human behavior.

Metcalf, Lawrence, editor. *Values Education: Rationale, Strategies, and Procedures.* 41st. Yearbook of the National Council for the Social Studies. Washington, D.C.: N.C.S.S.

A collection of readings on teaching values analysis. Emphasizes objectives, teaching strategies and procedures, and methods of resolving value conflicts.

Meux, Milton. *Strategies and Procedures for the Resolution of Value Conflict.* Salt Lake City: University of Utah, 1971.

Presents strategies for value conflict resolution.

Miller, Harry G., and Vinocur, Samuel M. "A Method of Clarifying Value Statements in the Social Studies Classroom: A Self-Instructional Program," 1972. ED 070 687.

A method of teacher response designed to aid in the analysis and clarification of value statements.

Moral Dilemmas of American Presidents: The Agony of Decision. New York: Pathescope Educational Films, 1974.

Five color-filmstrips with sound which stimulate values analysis.

Nelson, Jack L., editor. *American Values Series: Challenges and Choices.* Rochelle Park, N.J.: Hayden, 1974–1975.

Using a format of case studies and divergent viewpoints, contemporary issues are discussed using inquiry, decision-making, and values analysis. 14 titles. A teacher's guide: *An Introduction to Value Inquiry: A Student Process Book* is also available.

Newmann, Fred M., with Oliver, Donald W. *Clarifying Public Controversy: An Approach to Teaching Social Studies.* Boston: Little, Brown & Co., 1970.

Presents rationale and teaching strategies for clarifying value statements and public policy issues.

Oliver, Donald, and Newmann, Fred, editors. *Harvard Social Studies Project: The Public Issues Series.* Middletown, Conn.: Xerox Educational Publications, 1967–1974.

Case studies offer students value judgments to make on vital social issues.

Oliver, Donald W., and Shaver, James P. *Teaching Public Issues in the High School.* Boston: Houghton Mifflin, 1966.

Theory and strategies for rational discussion of issues of public controversy. Value strategies are stressed.

Olmo, Barbara. "A Process of Values Analysis." *The Social Studies.* Vol. 66, No. 2, pp. 72–75.

Describes values analysis theory and practice.

Politics and Morality. Middletown, Conn.: Xerox Educational Publications.

Case studies focus on value dilemmas faced by elected officials and candidates for public office.

Ruggiero, Vincent Ryan. *The Moral Imperative: Ethical Issues for Discussion and Writing.* Port Washington, N.Y.: Alfred Publishing Co., 1973.

12 case dilemmas are presented on topics of education, medias, sex, government, business, medicine, war, science, and law for student discussion and composition.

Scriven, Michael. *Student Values as Educational Objectives.* Boulder, Colo.: Social Science Education Consortium, 1966.

A strong rationale is presented for the teaching of value-reasoning.

_____. "Values and the Valuing Process." Orinda, Calif.: Diablo Valley Education Project, 1971.

Paper develops a basic conceptual framework for the rational evaluation of values and the valuing process.

Shaver, James P. *Facing Value Decisions: Rationale Building for Teachers.* Belmont, Calif.: Wadsworth, 1976.

A good source for understanding the place of values in teaching and alternative approaches to teaching values. Emphasis is placed on values analysis.

Shaver, James, and Larkins, A. Guy. *The Analysis of Public Issues Program.* Boston, Mass.: Houghton-Mifflin, 1973.

Multi-media program which engages students in values analysis and recognition and resolution of values conflict.

Values and Decisions. Middletown, Conn.: Xerox Education Publications.

An American history series focusing on a critical human/political decision. Students examine human/political values.

Role-Playing for Social Values

Fannie and George Shaftel[141] have explained role-playing theory and have designed role-playing exercises that encourage students and teachers to gain insight into values and feelings, and to establish an empathetic identification with characters. (Role-playing requires individuals to take on and act out the roles of real or imaginary characters in various situations.) The purpose of role-playing is to involve children in a situation in which there is a conflict between two or more values. The focus of role-playing is upon "educating for ethical behaviors and specifically for individual integrity and group responsibility."[142] The Shaftels believe that through role-playing, personal values emerge as students experience decision-making. They state:

> Through role-playing of typical conflict situations, children and young people can be helped to articulate the ways in which they tend to solve their problems. In the enactments, the consequences (social and personal) of the choices they make become more explicit. Analyses of these choices can lay bare the values underlying each line of action. Young people can thus learn that they act (make decisions) on the basis of the values they hold, which may be consciously, but most often are unconsciously, held. Once aware of their own valuing, they are in a position to modify their values.[143]

To engage students in role-playing, the teacher reads a story (or shows a film, plays a record, etc.) which deals with an open-ended situation designed to involve the viewer in the dilemma of a value conflict. The teacher guiding the role-playing should remain non-evaluative, supportive, and an active listener for the underlying meaning of what the students are saying. The teacher's role is to involve the children in exploring their own feelings as well as those of the characters, and to look at ways people may react to a given situation. Little time is involved in planning so that action remains spontaneous and uninhibited. The dialogue is not planned.

The role-playing dramatizes what the consequences of a given decision will be. A discussion follows the role-playing which may lead to replaying a revised or new role situation. During the discussion, the students should define the problem, consider alternative actions, weigh the consequences of each choice, and make a decision. It is important not to evaluate the quality of performance. Instead the teacher can focus on how real the enactment was, what ideas and feelings were presented, and what will happen next.

The teaching technique is to establish an empathetic identification with the characters in conflict. By so doing, the students are able to explore the value conflict involved and propose solutions. The procedure for role-playing is described in the following steps:

1. "Warming up" the group (problem confrontation). Through discussion, or stopping a story at a crucial point, or through a dramatic incident, stimulate the group so that they want to learn the best ways to cope with a situation.

2. Selecting the participants (role-players). Sensitize the children to their roles by telling them that they will be asked to take parts.

3. Preparing the audience to participate as observers. Remind the children that they will have opportunities to replay the situation, and that they are looking only at roles, not at the child personally.

4. Setting the stage. Role-players very briefly plan what they are going to do.

5. Role-playing (enactment).

6. Discussing and evaluating. During the discussion have the children define the problem, consider alternative action, weigh the consequences of each choice, discuss the values on which each alternative is based, and decide as to the best alternative.

7. Further enactments. Replaying revised roles, playing suggested next steps, or exploring alternative possibilities.

8. Further discussion.

9. Sharing experiences.[144]

MONEY FOR MARTY

"Money for Marty" is one of the problem-solving stories for role-playing created by the Shaftels. This open-ended situation is designed to involve students in a dilemma of conflicting values—integrity vs. revenge. The story is preceded by a statement of the problem and suggestions for introducing the situation.

> The problem: The issue is honesty: if someone has cheated you, is it fair to cheat him in return? Bryan owes Marty fifty cents he has borrowed but not paid back in spite of Marty's repeated requests. Marty has a chance to get his money back—by stealing it in a way that will cause Bryan much trouble.
>
> Introducing the problem: Say to the group, "Have you ever lent something to a friend—who just never gets around to giving it back? If you have, you can remember how provoked you felt. This story is about such a happening. The story stops but is not finished. As I read, think of ways in which you might end the story."

Marty had put his foot on a shiny half dollar.

Nearby, on hands and knees, Bryan was searching through the grass, carefully parting the blades to peer between them for a silvery telltale glint.

"Marty, help me?" he pleaded. "I lost my half dollar!"

"Too bad," Marty said, "Too bad you didn't pay me what you owe me before you lost that money."

"Oh, I couldn't pay you out of *that* half dollar!"

"Oh, no?" Well, you are a chum, you are, Marty said to himself. He was really disgusted with Bryan. He had lent Bryan two bits for a movie just a week before, when Bryan already owed him for a hot dog and a coke. But Bryan who was good at mooching always managed to forget any debts he owed.

"I couldn't pay you from that half dollar," Bryan explained, "because it isn't mine. Besides it's special. It's a coin from my Dad's collection. I brought it to school to show it to Mr. Dolan. He collects coins. I didn't tell my Dad I was taking it. He doesn't like me to mess with his collection. Besides, this coin isn't worth just fifty cents. It's scarce, so it's worth a lot more. Dad'll really be sore!"

So you're in trouble, Marty thought. Well, go ahead and squirm. You got it coming to you. Then Marty thought of Bryan's father. He'd really be rough on Bryan.

Marty almost lifted his foot, almost said, "Hey look—" but checked the impulse. Bryan needed a lesson.[145]

But this would be so tough a lesson. . . .

SELECTED BIBLIOGRAPHY OF SUPPORTING CURRICULUM MATERIALS FOR ROLE-PLAYING

Chester, M., and Fox, Robert. *Role-Playing Methods in the Classroom*. Chicago: Science Research Associates, 1966.

The booklet discusses the theoretical background for role-playing and gives a step-by-step discussion of how to use role-playing in the classroom.

Eiseman, Jeffrey W. *The Deciders*. Menlo Park, Calif.: Institute for Staff Development, 1969.

A teaching guide to decision-making for adolescents. Role playing is used extensively.

Grambs, Jean Dresden. *Intergroup Education: Methods and Materials*. Englewood Cliffs, N.J.: Prentice-Hall. 1968.

Hawley, Robert C. *Value Exploration Through Role-Playing* (Practical Strategies for Use in the Classroom). New York: Hart Publishing, 1975.

Role-playing techniques are applied in teaching subject matter, moral judgment, and decision-making.

LaRue, William; Larue, Sydney; and Hill, Shirley. *Understanding Our Feelings: An Adventure in Classroom Role Playing*. Chicago: Century Consultants, Combined Registry Co.

A series of stories directed for role-playing.

Quigley, Charles N., and Longlaker, Richard. *Voices for Justice: Role-Playing in Democratic Procedures*. Lexington, Mass.: Ginn, 1970.

Students act out decision-making processes inherent in a democratic society. Students clarify values in the eight case studies.

Rauch, Berna. *How Do You Feel? A Guidebook of Selected Activities for Teaching Human Relations.* Minneapolis, Minn.: T. S. Denison, 1973.

Twenty-four activities of the upper elementary and intermediate classroom to learn empathy and how others feel by putting themselves in the place of others.

Shaftel, Fannie, and Shaftel, George. *Role-playing for Social Values: Decision-making in the Social Studies.* Englewood Cliffs, N. J.: Prentice-Hall, 1967.

This book focuses on the use of role-playing to explore group behavior and the dilemmas of the child in the search for identity and personal values.

——————. *Values in Action.* Minneapolis, Minn.: Winston Press Inc.

This set of 10 filmstrips and recordings is suitable for discussions and role-playing to help students examine values. A teacher's guide and demonstration lesson accompany the set.

——————. *Values in Action: Role-Playing Problem-Situations for the Intermediate Grades.* New York: Holt, Rinehart, & Winston, 1970. Sound-filmstrips for discussion and roleplaying.

——————. *Values in Action: Role-Playing Problem Situations for the Intermediate Grades.* Los Angeles, Calif.: Churchill Films, 1969.

The value films are adapted from the book, *Role-Playing for Social Values,* and deal with open-ended situations which are designed to involve the viewer in the dilemmas of a value conflict. Titles are: (grades K–3) "A Bike," "The Hideout," "On Herbert Street," (grades 4–7) "Paper Drive," "Clubhouse Boat," "Trick or Treat."

——————. *Words and Action: Role-Playing for Young Children,* and *People in Action: Role-playing and Discussion Photographs for Elementary Social Studies.* New York: Holt, Rinehart, & Winston, 1970.

Understanding Our Feelings. San Rafael, Calif.: Leswing Press.

Kit contains 20 study prints to stimulate classroom role-playing on topics such as loneliness, learning friendship, work, and responsibility. Teacher's manual as a guide to role-playing is included.

Confluent Education

Confluent education is an approach to values education which combines the cognitive and affective domains in group and individual learning. George Isaac Brown, in his book, *Human Teaching for Human Learning,*[146] presents the concept of confluent education:

Confluent education is the term for the integration or flowing together of the *affective* and *cognitive* elements in individual and group learning. . .

Affective refers to the feeling or emotional aspect of experience and learning. How a child or adult feels about wanting to learn, how he feels as he learns, and what he feels after he has learned are included in the affective domain.

Cognitive refers to the activity of the mind in knowing an object, to intellectual functioning. What an individual learns and the intellectual process of learning it would fall within the cognitive domain—unless what is learned is an attitude or value, which would be affective learning.[147]

The confluence arises from the belief that there is no intellectual learning without some sort of feeling, and there are no feelings without the mind's being somehow involved.

Confluent education is rooted in the approaches and techniques of humanistic psychology and the human potential movement as applied to education. This approach has also been described as "humanistic education" by G. Weinstein and M. Fantini[148] and "process education" by Terry Borton.[149] In confluent education the cognitive and affective domains are integrated with regular curriculum goals and objectives as well as providing courses for special student needs.

The essential features of confluent education have been described by Stewart B. Shapiro in *The Live Classroom: Innovation through Confluent Education and Gestalt.*[150] The statements presented below are a summary of Shapiro's efforts to synthesize the techniques, concepts, values, and settings to provide a model for confluent education. They include:

1. Setting a classroom climate of two-way openness to learning. Setting such a climate includes awareness of the teacher's own values, patterns, and selective reinforcement of students' responses and behaviors.

2. Awareness by the teacher and students of themselves as legitimate objects of learning and applying deliberate attention to this learning.

3. Selection of subject matter in the classroom which is closely related to the significant personal needs and feelings of the students. The major reason for inclusion of any subject is the extent to which students can come to feel significantly related to it.

4. Experienced-based learning. This means learning that is closely tied to the direct contemporary experiences of students, and learning in which inferences and abstractions are drawn after the concrete learning experience itself.

5. Awareness and intention to develop convergent and *cognitive processes integrated with* action and will, as well as affect.

6. Encouragement of the expression of *feelings* by both student and teacher.

7. Use of *feedback* to refine and develop learnings.

8. Encouragement of divergent *imaginative thinking*.

9. "Re-subjectivising" of meanings. This involves the re-creation and internalizing of external, social, and transpersonal meanings, and perception and knowledge. Fantasy activities are designed to help people experience this transpersonal meaning by means of transforming symbols and active imagination.

In addition, George Brown has suggested two questions which can be helpful to teachers who desire to structure a more confluent approach to education:

1. How does the student feel *now* about the content of what I am teaching?

2. Is there any way to establish a relationship between this content and the student's life?[151]

Many of the confluent educational activities described by Weinstein and Fantini, Borton, and Brown can be integrated into traditional curricula and regular school programs. The student, through an exercise, real experience, or in reaction to a specific piece of material can develop skills in decision-making, problem-solving, and values clarification.

An example of a confluent education activity is a secondary school strategy entitled "Animal Fantasy."[152] This activity serves as a stimulus for students to discuss their feelings about themselves and others and to decide why they feel as they do. The students write the name of a person they dislike on a sheet of paper, the name of someone they like on a second sheet, and their own name on a third sheet. They then write the name of an animal this person most closely resembles. They affix a descriptive adjective before each animal and share with the group for trait comparisons and discussion.

Although the real names are not shared with the group, the introspection of both the reader and listener is interesting to observe. Sometimes, after discussion with the group an individual will realize that his or her choice was a prejudicial one or was based on some minor external characteristic of the individual.

Next, the students imagine what would happen if they were in a forest and met the despised animal, the loved animal, and the animal they feel the closest to. They write their own endings to these open-ended activities and again share and discuss them with the group. Activities like this combine values clarification together with creative listening and writing skills, discussion skills, and can lead to other language arts studies and activities.

A confluent activity conducted in an elementary setting is reported by Anita Cassarino in *The Live Classroom.*[153] The activity is part of a unit on plants, and the teacher is explaining mushrooms and molds. Here is how Cassarino describes the experience:

> The children then rotated to one of three areas to draw mushrooms, to view mold under a microscope and draw it, or to view and discuss mold growing in a jar. . .
> We discussed the fact that mold did not grow from seeds but that pieces of it floated in the air, and when they settled under favorable conditions, mold began to grow. I then asked for volunteers to think of a conversation that might occur between the food in the jar and the mold, Here are some examples:
> FOOD: You get off me.
> MOLD: No, I won't.
> F: I'm going to tell my mother.
> M: You go ahead and tell.
>
> F: You're not going to get on me, mold.
> M: Yes, I am.
> F: When you get on food, you look ugly.
>
> F: You can't get me' You can't get me!
> M: Yes I can. Gotcha!
> F: Ugh.
> An interesting thing happened when I introduced the conversation exercise with the first group that came to the jar. As one child was talking, a number of children working at other activities stopped what they were doing to come over and listen. A hush fell over the room.
> I felt that through the conversation between mold and food the children could grasp the dependency relationship better than if I had just stuck with scientific explanation. It also reinforced the idea that mold develops from something outside the plant.[154]

SELECTED BIBLIOGRAPHY OF SUPPORTING CURRICULUM MATERIALS FOR CONFLUENT EDUCATION

Bessell, Harold, and Palomares, Uvaldo. *The Human Development Program*. San Diego: Human Development Training Institute. 1970.

This approach (Magic Circle) includes a theory book, lesson guides for 180 activities, and rating scales.

Borton, Terry. *Reach, Touch, and Teach: Student Concerns and Process Education*. New York: McGraw-Hill, 1970.

Based on a project in "process education," Borton presents his own experiences in reaching children through their personal concerns while also teaching them cognitive skills in an organized way. From this experience he builds a psychological theory of education and suggestions for application.

Brown, George Isaac. *Human Teaching for Human Learning*. New York: Viking Press, 1971.

Brown presents projects in confluent education, which combine cognitive and affective learning. Book describes teacher training program and gives examples of projects in elementary and secondary classrooms.

Brown, George Isaac, editor, with Yeomans, Thomas, and Grizzard, Liles. *The Live Classroom*. New York: Viking Press, 1975.

A book of readings which describe many activities to involve the student in responsibility of the learning process. Many approaches to confluent education and Gestalt therapy are discussed as they apply from Grades 1–12.

Costillo, Gloria. *Left-Handed Teaching*. New York: Prager Publishers. 1974.

Part I describes a model that allows for the development of the whole child-affective as well as cognitive dimensions. Part II-lessons designed for affective education. Part III demonstrates the use and techniques of confluent education.

The Confluent Education Journal. Santa Barbara, Calif.: Confluent Education Development and Research Center.

Semiannual periodical dealing with all aspects of the theory and practice of confluent education.

Dinkmeyer, Don, editor. *AGS DUSO Program*. Circle Pines, Minn.: American Guidance Services, Inc. 1970.

A multi-media elementary school program designed to enable children to talk more freely about feelings, goals, values, and behavior.

Fantini, Mario, and Weinstein, Gerald. *Toward a Contact Curriculum*. New York: Anti-Defamation League of B'nai B'rith, 1969.

Presents a number of teaching strategies designed to bring together cognitive and affective learnings.

Jones, Richard M. *Fantasy and Feeling in Education.* New York: Harper & Row, 1968.

Proposes that education must include emotional issues as well as cognitive goals in order to fully involve students in learning.

Lederman, Janet. *Anger and the Rocking Chair.* New York: Viking Press, 1973.

A dramatic account of the use of Gestalt method with children in elementary schools.

Leonard, George. *Education and Ecstacy.* New York: Dell, 1968.

Describes practical suggestions for merging affective and cognitive learning based upon Leonard's observations of innovative schools, a brain-research laboratory, and experimental communities.

Lyon, Harold C., Jr. *Learning to Feel-Feeling to Learn.* Columbus, Ohio: Charles E. Merrill Publishing Co., 1971.

Comprehensive survey of people, theories, and techniques in the field of affective and humanistic education. There are also detailed examples of classroom applications.

Newberg, Norman, and Borton, Terry. *Education for Student Concerns.* Philadelphia: School District of Philadelphia, 1968. Affective Education Research Project.

Samples, Bob, and Wohlford, Bob. *Opening:* Menlo Park, Calif.: Addison-Wesley Publishing Co., 1973.

This book uses photographs and prose to elicit feelings, values, and attitudes about personal issues.

Sohn, David. *Come to Your Senses.* Englewood Cliffs, N. J.: Scholastic Book Services.

A series of four filmstrips and a teaching guide which are designed to increase students' awareness of themselves, others, and the world around them. A confluent approach.

Rubin, Louis J., editor. *Facts and Feelings in the Classroom.* New York: Viking Press. 1973.

Presents a process of teaching in which the affective and cognitive domains are treated co-equally in teaching and learning.

Weinstein, Gerald. "The Trumpet: A Guide to Humanistic Psychological Curriculum," *Theory Into Practice.* Vol. 13, No. 5, pp. 335–342.

Presents a strategy for selecting and sequencing affective activities.

Weinstein, Gerald, and Fantini, Mario, editors, *Toward Humanistic Education: A Curriculum of Affect*. New York: Praeger, 1970.

Based on a Ford Foundation project at the elementary level. Presents a conceptual model for humanistic teaching, some examples of specific techniques, and ways they were applied within the project.

Williams, F. E. *A Total Creativity Program for Individualizing and Humanizing the Learning Process*. Englewood Cliffs, N. J.: Educational Technology Publications. 1973.

Action Learning

The action learning approach to values education offers experiences for students to act directly in personal and social action related to their values. Douglas P. Superka claims that the distinguishing characteristic of the action learning approach is that it provides specific opportunities for students to act on their values. "That is, it does not confine values education to the classroom or group setting but extends it to experimental learning in the community, where the interplay between choices and actions is continuous and must be dealt with."[155]

Action learning encourages teachers and students to move beyond the classroom to school-based and community-based learning activities. Robert Barr[156] has described some of the types of action learning programs that exist: outdoor learning programs, cross-cultural exchange programs, service programs, internship programs, and travel experiences. Barr offers a number of suggestions to help organize these programs. These include course supplements, course replacements or equivalents, semester experiences, year-long experiences, adult/community education, external school experiences, and non-school learning experiences.

Fred M. Newmann, author of *Education for Citizen Action: Challenge for Secondary Curriculum*,[157] has argued for the teaching of a variety of skills and knowledge which should be promoted in action learning. These include knowledge of the political-legal process, advocacy skills, knowledge and skills in group dynamics, and practical skills in organization, administration, and management.

The potential growth in values as a result of action learning comes from the increased social interaction and role-taking opportunities experienced by students. Writing in the *74th Yearbook of National Society for the Study of Education*,[158] Richard Graham states:

The reasons that certain kinds of action-learning may have good and lasting effect is that they provide experience in taking on new roles in society, new perspectives that demand the exercise of a sophisticated logic of social interaction, and in doing so, stimulate basic changes in the structure of one's social perspective and moral judgment.[159]

Graham has delineated five stages of action-learning experiences which parallel Kohlberg's moral development stages. Graham's claim is that some experiences will predictably create the personal advancement to higher stages of moral development. Hence, the success of action-learning experiences depends upon the nature of the match between an individual's social and moral development and the nature of the action-learning experience. Graham's action-learning stages are summarized briefly below:

Stage 1 —Carrying out orders in prescribed ways as in well-defined, military assignments; some fixed-rate production or assembly work. (Rules are to be obeyed, Stage 1, Kohlberg)

Stage 2 —Piece-rate jobs, e.g. fruit picking at so much a basket, some sales clerk assignments, some assignments helping others. (One's responsibility is for self and, in part, for others, Stage 2, Kohlberg)

Stage 3 —Group work as at some hamburger stands, secretaries in a pool, some kinds of sales work, some shared production work or group bench work, some responsibilities for helping others, e.g., child care. (One's desire is to do one's share and be liked by peers, employers, or the persons served, Stage 3, Kohlberg)

Stage 4 —Carrying out responsibilities in the absence of group support. Some supervisory or instructional assignments. Some kinds of legal or correctional work. Some sales work involving the influencing of others. Some assignments helping others. (One's concern is for self and others, to do one's duty according to rules and convention, Stage 4, Kohlberg)

Stage 5 —Positions of decision-making in the presence of conflict. Some personnel work or counseling; some work involving responsibilities for others; negotiated policy formation and decision-making, some legislative work, negotiating goals and standards, cooperatively establishing or revising rules and procedures in light of underlying principles. (One's concern is for self and others according to fundamental principles of fairness and utility.)[160]

The teaching of action learning activities uses methods and techniques of the various approaches to values education discussed earlier. However, in planning and organizing action learning projects, techniques and skills in group organization and interpersonal relations are important.[161]

Many of the existing action learning activies which are included in curriculum materials give students opportunities to participate in performing tasks and making decisions that confront social problems. (Stages 4 and 5 of Graham.) Activities may stress personal awareness and personal growth such as community service programs, or action learning activities may strive for social change within the community by having students engage in political or legislative experiences. These experiences are frequently developed as course supplements to regular classroom work or as a component for a particular course.

Examples of four action learning projects have been reported by Fred M. Newmann[162] and are described below:

1. Group A wishes to protect land surrounding a glacial pond from development into a high-rise apartment complex. The developer, who has already purchased the land, has requested that the city council change the zoning from single family to high-rise apartments so that construction may begin. Group A decides to do all it can to prevent this change in zoning.

2. Group B wants to help students in trouble with the law. After visiting various juvenile detention facilities, it decides to make weekly visits to a state detention center for boys, spending an hour playing cards, dancing, and talking.

3. Group C wants to form a Black Students' union to increase communication and a sense of community among Blacks scattered in four different high schools. They decide to publish a student newspaper and to promote a cultural festival. They want to attract more Blacks into their organization and to learn of their heritage through films, speakers, and books which have not been previously available in school.

4. Mike, a high school student, wants to learn something about courts and the legal profession. He arranges an internship with the clerk of a local judge. Mike spends several hours each week

observing courtroom procedures, discussing this with the clerk, and occasionally with the judge. The clerk helps to explain the operation of the system and reasons for the judge's decision.[163]

"Sensitivity modules" are another form of action learning activities. Howard Kirschenbaum[164] has designed these activities as short experiences to increase student's awareness of social issues. Some of the suggested activities are:

> Wear old clothes and sit in the waiting room of the State Employment Office. Listen, observe, talk to some of the people sitting next to you. Read the announcements on the bulletin board, etc.

> Go to an inner-city elementary school and read a story to a child in kindergarten or first grade. The child must be held in your lap.

> Spend a few hours in a prowl car traveling with a team of police. Listen to the squad car radio. Ask questions. If police park and walk a beat, walk with them.

> Live for three days on the amount of money a typical welfare mother receives to feed a son or daughter closest to your own age.[165]

SELECTED BIBLIOGRAPHY OF SUPPORTING CURRICULUM MATERIALS FOR ACTION LEARNING

Action Learning Schools. Washington, D.C.: National Association of Secondary School Principles, 1974.

Background readings and description of 25 action learning programs.

Arms, Myron, and Denman, David. *Touching the World: Adolescents, Adults and Action Learning.* New York: Charles Scribner & Sons, 1975.

Describes Philadelphia "Kaleidoscope" program designed to provide community experiences that enable students to pursue their personal goals.

Aronstein, Laurence, and Olsen, Edward G. *Action Learning: Student Community Service Project.* Washington, D.C.: Association for Supervision and Curriculum Development, 1974.

Provides an organizational structure for action learning programs including selection, implementation, and evaluation.

Barr, Robert D. "The Development of Action Learning Programs." *NASSP Bulletin*, May 1976, pp. 106–109.

Provides ideas for action learning programs and organizational structures.

Forty Projects by Groups of Kids. New York: National Commission on Resources for Youth, Inc., 1973. ED 093 786.

Description and identification of action learning experiences.

Graham, Richard, "Youth and Experiential Learning." Havighurst and Dreyer (ed), *Youth: 74th. Yearbook of the National Society for the Study of Education.* (Edited by Robert J. Havighurst.) Chicago: University of Chicago, 1975. pp. 161–912.

Presents a rationale for action learning and relates action learning to moral development.

High School Courses with Volunteer Components. National Student Volunteer Program/Action, Washington, D.C.: Superintendent of Documents, U.S. Government Printing Office, 1974.

Describes case studies of high school courses that use volunteer activities to complement classroom learning.

High School Student Volunteers. National Student Volunteer Program/Action. Washington, D.C.: Superintendent of Documents, U.S. Government Printing Office, 1974.

Suggests guidelines for establishing and maintaining student volunteer programs.

Jones, W. Ron. *Finding Community: A Guide to Community Research and Action.* Palo Alto, Calif.: James E. Freed, 1971.

A practical guide for community action learning and value activities.

Kirschenbaum, Howard. "Sensitivity Modules." *Humanistic Education Sourcebook.* (Edited by Donald A. Read and Sidney B. Simon.) Englewood Cliffs, N.J.: Prentice-Hall, 1975. pp. 315–320.

Introduces a number of values clarifying activities which are to be conducted within the community. Many activities are observation or participant observation of nature, desired to increase awareness.

New Roles for Youth in the School and the Community. The National Commission on Resources for Youth/forward by Ralph Tyler, chairman. Englewood Cliffs, N. J.: Scholastic, 1974.

Case histories of nearly 70 of the most effective youth-social action programs. Guidelines and strategies for implementation are included.

Newmann, Fred, M. *Education for Citizen Action: Challenge for Secondary Curriculum.* Berkeley, Calif.: McCutchan Publishing Co., 1975.

Presents the rationale and purpose of action learning; discusses the competencies of action learning; and relates action learning to teaching and curriculum development.

Newmann, Fred, M. "Student Intentions in Social Action Projects," *Social Science Education Consortium Newsletter*. No. 12, Feb., 1972.

Description of projects and student attitudes toward social action projects. Segment on implication for teaching is included.

Newmann, Fred M., and Oliver, Donald. *Social Action: Dilemmas and Strategies*, an AEP Public Issues Series booklet. Middletown, Conn.: Xerox Corporation, 1972.

Presents case studies of young people involved in social action. A values analysis approach to discussion is used. Community action activities are suggested.

Values Education Series. Evanston, Ill.: McDougal, Littell, and Co. 1975.

Each book contains a series of moral cases and process activities which call for student values clarification and decision-making. In addition, community action activities are suggested. Titles are: *Deciding on the Human Use of Power, Deciding How To Live on Spaceship Earth, Deciding How To Live as Society's Children, Deciding How To Act in a Political Society, and Teacher's Guide to the Values Education Series*, by Rodney F. Allen.

6. Evaluating Student Outcomes

The evaluation of student progress is one of the most important and controversial activities conducted by schools. The task of evaluating student outcomes as a result of values instruction is a sensitive area, at best. If the purpose of evaluation is to measure whether student competencies improved as a result of instruction,[166] how can or should teachers assess students' moral development, attitudes, beliefs, or values?

The difficulty here is two-fold: First, "while knowledge . . . has been regarded as public and worthy of reward and acclaim, attitudes, values, beliefs, and personal commitments have been regarded as private matters in our society. . . . Public school educators face legitimate restrictions whenever they seek to alter student attitudes, values, or commitments."[167] Secondly, there is the problem of the use of evaluation as indoctrination. J. A. Sweeney and J. B. Parsons explain:

> If the teacher evaluates students by testing them on the content of their values after implying an open-inquiry process, students will quickly and correctly assume that it is the same old game of looking for 'right' answers only in a new way. If close-ended evaluation procedures are used after the first controversial social issues discussion, the teacher can feel reasonably sure that future discussions will not succeed.[168]

Rodney Allen[169] has laid out a defensible evaluation system for values instruction divided into short-term and long-term assessment techniques. He advocates two short-term methods of evaluation: (1) careful teacher observation of student performance in class activities and discussions, and (2) the teacher's use of probing questions in class discussions to reveal changes and improved reasoning ability. Long-term methods of assessment include: (1) audio-taping or video-taping class discussions on a variety of issues throughout the course for shared evaluation between teacher and student, and (2) examining written essays or other assignments to accumulate a record of student development.

Richard and Gerri Curwin[170] have stated that the teacher's responsibility in evaluating values clarification activities is to provide opportunities for it to take place and to supply appropriate tools. The Curwins urge teachers to allow for student self-evaluation by implementing the following techniques: (1) asking "central questions" (these are probing, clarifying questions), (2) asking students to keep a journal of "I learned statements," "I felt statements," or positions on values issues, and (3) having students participate in a long-term classroom project.

A number of assessment instruments and guides have been developed to measure an individual's level of moral reasoning along Kohlberg's stages of moral development. Although Kohlberg has not published his scoring manuals used to conduct moral judgment interviews, N. Porter and N. Taylor[171] have published a guide for teachers who seek to measure the degree of moral development reached by their students. The Defining Issues Test,[172] developed by James Rest, is a paper and pencil test which also measures moral judgment along Kohlberg's stages.

	Kerry	Missy	Clint	Eric	Janey	Mark	Ann
Morality of Constraint							
Duty is obeying authorities.	X	X	X	X		X	X
Good is defined by obedience to rules.	X	X	X	X		X	X
Rules or laws are not analyzed.	X					X	
The letter of the law is followed.	X		X	X		X	
Forbidden behavior results in anxiety.		X					
Violation of game rules produces concern.	X		X	X	X		X
Justice is punitive.	X	X	X			X	
Any transgression is considered serious.	X	X		X	X		X
Responsibility is viewed objectively.	X	X					X
Intentions are not considered.	X			X	X		X
Egocentrism dominates.	X	X	X		X		X
Judgments are made in conformity to the law.	X	X	X	X	X		X
Morality of Cooperation							
Control is established by mutual agreement.							
Lessening of adult constraint occurs.			X			X	
Rules can be modified.				X			
Justice is viewed as restitutive.		X		X			
Concern for inequalities develops.					X		
Concern for social injustices develops.					X		
The spirit of the law is considered.							X
Responsibility is viewed subjectively.							X
Motives are considered.		X				X	
Rights to opinions are respected.			X			X	
Judgments include motives and intentions.				X			

X means characteristic of.

Kerry, Eric, Janey and Ann might be grouped together for instruction to help them expand their viewpoints or perceptions to include the rights of others to form their own opinions (characteristic of morality of cooperation). Clint and Mark might be added to the group to provide some additional insight as to the acceptance of the opinions of others.

FIG. 3—"Diagnostic-prescriptive checksheet for moral development" from "Moral Education through Diagnostic-prescriptive Teaching Methods" by Trudi Annette Fulda and Richard Kieth Jantz, *The Elementary School Journal*, May, 1975, p. 516.

T. A. Fulda and R. K. Jantz[173] have recommended the use of a check sheet as an efficient way to analyze students' moral development (see Figure 3). The skills found on the check list are derived from Piaget's[174] stages of moral development. Jantz and Fulda have utilized these stages as a general framework of sequencing moral skills. The diagnosis of a child's level of moral development serves as a springboard for the teaching of moral development. In planning lessons for children, the teacher can expose students to situations in which they are experiencing conflict in making moral decisions and then engage students in a higher stage of moral reasoning.

7.   Structure of the School and Values Education

Thus far, most of the focus on teaching values education has been on the substantive, planned curriculum which is brought to the attention of the student. The role of the teacher has been characterized as providing structure for values education activities, such as supplying curriculum materials, organizing time, giving directions, conducting discussions, and facilitating interactions. Yet, perhaps the greatest source of value teaching is derived from the actual structure and organization of the school.

Values education cannot be discussed without some understanding of the purpose, content, and structure of the institution within which it is to be taught. The school as an institution contains many implicit assumptions and premises which can enhance or detract from a program in values education. Barry Sugarman has presented a dynamic picture of the school as a "fluid system in which a variety of actors with different interests and resources work out their relationships within the framework of an official structure."[175] These actors include not only teachers, students, principals, and parents, but also the more diffuse agencies of peer group, culture, and school rules and regulations. In other words, no matter how well meaning a teacher may be, many values are transmitted covertly, or indirectly, as a result of the institutional norms within which one works.

Several studies have addressed the manner in which the overall organization or structure of the school influence the moral development and values of children. Robert Dreebeen's[176] analysis of what is learned in school proposes that school experience is structured so that children acquire values and attitudes that facilitate their integration into the competitive, occupational and political worlds of adults. Phillip Jackson's[177] observational studies of routine elementary school classrooms document the major elements of school life: the crowds, the praise, and the power. William G. Spady[178] has written that the school's emphasis on formal achievement, interpersonal competition, and certification strongly suggests how it may act to select students for the occupational, economic, and prestige structures of the society.

Finally, Joseph Grannis[179] has pointed out that school in general could be classified into a rough typology, namely, family schools, factory schools, and corporation schools. The latter two models are by far the predominant mode for schools in this country. What students are really learning in school, according to Grannis, are such organizational values as order, routine, output, authority, and efficiency. Schools are competing within human values and laying too little emphasis on individualization, self-development, personal relationships, due process, justice, and equality.

Unfortunately, in educational systems run on broadly authoritarian lines, the necessary relationship of mutual trust, respect, and cooperation among students and teachers is extremely difficult to cultivate. One may easily be forced into indoctrination by the authority structure within which one works. R. D. Hess and J. V. Torney,[180] in an empirical study, conclude that public school teachers tend to focus upon the importance of authority, the obedience to law, and conformity to school regulations at the expense of processes more characteristic of an intellectually oriented environment.

I have been focusing attention on what is called the "hidden curriculum" and its manifestations in schools. The hidden curriculum includes a wide range of learnings—attitudinal, emotional, moral, and social—of what is really learned from the ways in which the school environment is organized. The hidden curriculum is in contrast to the overt, formal curriculum which consists of what goes on in formal class instruction. Clive Beck[181] has summarized the tensions and conflicts between the hidden curriculum and values education, when he states:

> Our experience in two high schools made us aware of the "hidden curriculum" discussed by critics of the school. We became much more sensitive to how the structure of the school can implicitly encourage a certain kind of morality—to be more specific, an authoritarian, conventional one.[182]

Lawrence Kohlberg,[183] Peter Scharf,[184] Edwin Fenton,[185] and others are experimenting with setting up "just" classroom and school environments to enhance the level of institutional justice. Kohlberg has argued that "if you want to develop morality or a sense of justice in kids, you have to create a just school, a just environment."[186] He describes the "Just Community School" as an attempt to engage students in democratic decision-making and to stimulate them in both moral reasoning and moral action within a just institution.[187]

Conclusion

Everyone has some world outlook, global view, and sense of values which may be tacit and unreflective. By educating the whole person and making the search for values an integral part of the curriculum, schools can create opportunities for students to make choices and decisions in all areas of human activity. The role of the teacher in developing values is to provide opportunities and experiences for students in which to formulate, clarify, or analyze personal and social values. Teachers can encourage the students' analysis of conflicting values, and allow students to affirm and defend value judgments and commitments.

Values education can meet the needs of learners in a time when social, economic, and political values are in a permanent state of confusion and change. The growth of science and technology, the declining influence of family and religious values, the acknowledgment of government corruption, and the alienation of many young people are among the factors which combine to make values education not only significant, but urgent. Perhaps Sidney Simon has said it best:

> At the root of what is wrong with today's children and our own lives as well is a colossal vacuum in the whole realm of values. Almost none of us has a clear idea of what we want, where we are going, why we are going there, who is going with us, and even who we are . . . I feel more and more strongly that in fighting our malaise the most severe problem facing all of us is HOW TO GET PEOPLE TO LOOK AT THE LIVES THEY ARE LEADING.[188]

99

References

1. Purpel, David, and Ryan, Kevin. "Moral Education: Where Sages Fear to Tread." *Phi Delta Kappan*, Vol. 56, No. 10, June 1975, pp. 659–662.
2. Barr, Robert D., editor. *Values and Youth*. Washington, D.C.: National Council for the Social Studies, 1971, p. 14.
3. *Ibid.*, p. 19.
4. Toffler, Alvin. *Future Shock*. New York: Bantam Books, Random House, Inc., 1971.
5. *Ibid.*, p. 463.
6. Kurtz, Paul. "Why Moral Education?" *The Humanist* Vol. 32, No. 6, November/December 1972. p. 5.
7. "American Schools: Whatever Happened to Ethics?" *The Christian Science Monitor*. April 15, 1976. pp. 14–15.
8. "Moral Education." *Newsweek*. March 1, 1976. pp. 74–75.
9. Johnson, David W. "Affective Education," *The Elementary School Journal*. Vol. 73, No. 6, March 1973. p. 306.
10. Fraenkel, Jack R. *Helping Students Think and Value*. Englewood Cliffs, N.J.: Prentice-Hall, Inc., 1973. p. 229.
11. Barr, *op. cit.*, p. 21.
12. Harmin, Merrill, and Simon, Sidney B. "Values." *The Teacher's Handbook*. (Edit. by Dwight W. Allen and Eli Seifman.) Glenview, Ill.: Scott, Foresman, and Co., 1971. pp. 691, 692, 693.
13. Fraenkel, *op. cit.*, p. 229.
14. Harmin and Simon, *op. cit.*, p. 693.
15. Kohlberg, Lawrence. "Development of Moral Character and Moral Ideology." *Review of Child Development Research*. Vol. 1. (Edited by M. L. Hoffman and L. W. Hoffman.) New York: Russell Sage Foundation, 1964. pp. 383–431.
16. Rogers, Carl R. *Freedom to Learn*. Columbus, Ohio: Charles E. Merrill Pub. Co., 1969. p. 239.
17. Rokeach, Milton. *The Nature of Human Values*. New York: The Free Press, 1973.
18. *Ibid.*, p. 8.
19. Fraenkel, Jack. "Strategies for Developing Values." *Today's Education*. Vol. 63, No. 7, Nov./Dec. 1973. p. 49.
20. Raths, Louis; Harmin, Merrill; and Simon, Sidney B. *Values and Teaching*. Columbus, Ohio: Charles E. Merrill Pub. Co., 1966.
21. *Ibid.*, p. 30.
22. Rogers, *op. cit.*
23. *Ibid.*, p. 242.
24. Lasswell, Harold. *The World Revolution of Our Time*. Stanford, Calif.: Stanford University Press, 1951.
25. Arnspiger, Robert H., "Education in Human Values." *School and Community*. Vol. 57, May 1972. pp. 16–17.
26. Krathwohl, David R., and Bloom, Benjamin S. *Taxonomy of Educational Objectives: Handbook II: Affective Domain*. New York: David McKay Co. Inc., 1964.
27. *Ibid.*, pp. 176–185.

28. Wilson, John; Williams, Norman; and Sugarman, Barry. *Introduction to Moral Education*. London: Penguin Books, 1967.
29. *Ibid.*, pp. 192–197.
30. Kohlberg, *op. cit.*
31. Kohlberg, Lawrence. "Developmental and Education Psychology," *Educational Psychologist*. Vol. 10, No. 1, Winter 1972, p. 6.
32. Kohlberg, Lawrence. "The Claim to Moral Adequacy of a Highest Stage of Moral Judgment." *The Journal of Philosophy*. Vol. 70, No. 18, Oct. 25, 1973. pp. 361–362.
33. See Freud, Sigmund. "On Narcissism: An Introduction." *Standard Edition*. Vol. 14, London: Hogarth Press, 1957. (Originally published in 1915.) *Beyond the Pleasure Principle: Standard Edition*. Vol. 18. London: Hogarth Press, 1955. (Originally published in 1920.)
34. Stone, Norma K. "The Development of Moral Thought in Children" in *Values, Feelings and Morals: Part I - Research and Perspectives*. Washington, D.C.: American Association of Elementary-Kindergarten-Nursery Educators, 1974. p. 5.
35. Erikson, Erik. *Childhood and Society*. New York: W. W. Norton and Co., 1950.
36. Hall, Robert T., and Davis, John U. *Moral Education in Theory and Practice*. Buffalo, N.Y.: Prometheus Books, 1975. p. 87.
37. Erikson, *op.cit.*, pp. 247–274.
38. Aronfreed, J. *Conduct and Conscience*. New York: Academic Press, 1968.
39. Bandura, A., and Walters, R. H. *Social Learning and Personality Development*. New York: Holt, Rinehart, & Winston, 1963.
40. Hoffman, M. L. "Moral Development." *Carmichael's Manual of Child Psychology* Vol. 2 (3rd edition). (Edited by P. H. Mussen.) New York: John Wiley and Sons, Inc. 1970. pp. 261–359.
41. Bandura, A., and McDonald, F. J. "The Influence of Social Reinforcement and the Behavior of Models in Shaping Children's Moral Judgments." *Journal of Abnormal and Social Psychology* Vol. 67, 1963. pp. 274–281.
42. Miller, N. E., and Dollard, J. *Social Learning and Imitation*. New Haven: Yale University Press, 1941.
43. Mischel, Walter, "Preference for Delayed Reinforcement and Social Responsibility." *Journal of Abnormal Social Psychology* Vol. 62, 1961. pp. 1–7.
44. Sears, R. R.; Rau, Lucy; and Alpert, R. *Identification and Child Rearing*. Stanford, Calif.: Stanford University Press, 1965.
45. Walters, R. H., and Demkow, L. "Timing of Punishment as a Determinant of Response Inhibition." *Child Development* Vol. 34, pp. 207–214.
46. Wright, Derek. *The Psychology of Moral Behavior*. Baltimore: Penguin Books, 1971. p. 39.
47. Piaget, Jean. *The Moral Judgment of the Child*. New York: The Free Press, 1965. (Originally published in 1932.)
48. Kohlberg, *op.cit.*

49. Adkins, D.C.; Payne, F.D.; and O'Malley, J. M., "Moral Development." *Review of Research in Education Vol. 2.* Itasca, Ill.: F. E. Peascock Pub. Inc., 1974. p. 110.

50. Piaget, *op.cit.*

51. Selman, Robert, "The Relation of Role-Taking to the Development of Moral Judgment in Children." *Child Development* Vol. 42, No. 1, 1974. pp. 79–91.

52. Schleifer, Michael. "Moral Education and Indoctrination," *Ethics* Vol. 86, No. 2, Jan. 1976. p. 156.

53. Fenton, Edwin. "Moral Education: The Research Findings." *Social Education* Vol. 40, No. 4, April 1976. pp. 188–193.

54. Crabtree, Walden, "A Clarification of the Teacher's Role in Moral Education," *Religious Education* Vol. 69, No. 6, Nov./Dec. 1974. p. 645.

55. Kachaturoff, Grace. "Teaching Values in the Public Schools." *The Social Studies* Vol. 64, No. 5, Oct. 1973. p. 226.

56. Soar, Robert. "Teacher Behavior and Pupil Growth." *Developing Value Constructs in Schooling: Inquiry into Process and Product.* (Edited by James A. Phillips, Jr.) Worthington, Ohio: Ohio Association for Curriculum and Supervision Development, 1972. pp. 28–40.

57. Curwin, R. L., and Curwin, G. *Developing Individual Values in the Classroom.* Palo Alto: Learning Handbooks, 1974.

58. Raths, Simon, and Harmin, *op.cit.*, p. 168.

59. Ryals, R., and Foster, D. "Classroom Climate and Value Teaching." *Education* Vol. 95, No. 4, 1974. pp. 354–359.

60. *Ibid.*, p. 354.

61. Howe, L. W., and Howe, M. M. *Personalizing Education: Values Clarification and Beyond.* New York: Hart Pub. Co., Inc., 1975.

62. Kohlberg, Lawrence, with Whitten, Phillip. "Understanding the Hidden Curriculum." *Learning* Vol. 1, No. 2, 1972. pp. 10–14.

63. Beck, Clive. *Moral Education in the Schools: Some Practical Suggestions.* Toronto: The Ontario Institute for Studies in Education, 1971. p. 20.

64. Allen, Rodney F. *Teaching Guide to the Plover Books.* Winona, Minn.: St. Mary's College Press, 1974. p. 69.

65. Bernstein, J.; Tannebaum, M.; Chase, L.; and Yeagle, G. "Examining Values in the Upper Grades." *Social Education* Vol. 35, No. 8, Dec. 1971. p. 906.

66. Wolfson, Bernice. "Values and the Primary School Teacher." *Social Education* Vol. 31, No. 1, Jan. 1967. p. 37.

67. Evans, Clyde. "Facing Up to Values." *Teacher.* Dec. 1974. p. 18.

68. Ezer, Melvin. "Value Teaching in the Middle and Upper Grades: A Rationale for Teaching But Not Transmitting Values." *Social Education* Vol. 31, No. 1, Jan. 1967. p. 39.

69. See Harmin, M.; Simon, S. B.; and Kirschenbaum, H. *Clarifying Values Through Subject Matter.* Minneapolis, Minn.: Winston Press, 1973.

70. Beck, *op.cit.*

71. Howe and Howe, *op.cit.* p. 26.

72. See Hawley, R. C., and Hawley, I. L. *Human Values in the Classroom: A Handbook for Teachers.* New York: Hart Pub. Co. Inc., 1975.

73. Ruchlis, H., and Sharefkin, B. *Reality-Centered Learning.* Englewood Cliffs, N.J.: Citation Press, 1975. p. 145.

74. Walsh, Huber M., editor. *An Anthology of Readings in Elementary Social Studies.* Washington, D.C.: National Council for the Social Studies, 1971. p. 73.

75. Shaver, J. P., and Strong, W. *Facing Value Decisions: Rationale-building for Teachers.* Belmont, Calif.: Wadsworth Pub. Co., 1976.

76. *Ibid.* p. 84.

77. Sadker, Mary and David. "Microteaching for Affective Skills." *The Elementary School Journal.* Nov. 1975. pp. 91–99.

78. Pine, G. J., and Boy, A. V., "Teaching and Valuing." *The Clearing House* Vol. 49, March 1976. p. 314.

79. Raths, Simon, and Harmin, *op.cit.*

80. Harmin, Simon, and Kirschenbaum, *op.cit.*, pp. 18–30.

81. Raths, Simon, and Harmin, *op.cit.*, p. 30.

82. *Ibid.*, pp. 30–33.

83. *Ibid.*, pp. 63–65.

84. Simon, S. B.; Howe, L.; and Kirschenbaum, H. *Values Clarification: A Handbook of Practical Strategies for Teachers and Students.* New York: Hart Pub. Co., 1972. p. 15.

85. *Ibid.*, p. 174.

86. *Ibid.*, p. 38.

87. *Ibid.*, p. 30.

88. *Ibid.*, p. 278.

89. Superka, D. P.; Ahrens, C.; and Hedstrom, J. E., with Ford, L. J., and Johnson, P. L. *Values Education Sourcebook: Conceptual Approaches, Materials Analyses, and an Annotated Bibliography.* Boulder, Colo.: Social Science Education Consortium, 1976. p. 7.

90. *Ibid.*

91. Rucker, W. R.; Arnspiger, V. C.; and Brodbeck, A. *Human Values in Education.* Dubuque, Iowa: Kendall/Hunt Pub. Co., 1969.

92. Simpson, Bert K. *Becoming Aware of Values.* San Diego, Calif.: Pennant Press, 1974.

93. Arnspiger, V. C.; Brill, J. A.; and Rucker, W. R. *Thinking with Values.* Teachers edition. Austin: Steck-Vaughn Co., 1973. p. 1.

94. Simpson, Bert K. *Becoming Aware of Values: A Resource Guide in the Use of Value Games.* San Diego: Pennant Press, 1972. pp. 14–15.

95. *Character Education Curriculum.* San Antonio: American Institute for Character Education, 1974.

96. *Ibid.*

97. Hill, Russell C. "Freedom's Code." *Character Education Journal* Vol. 2, No. 3, Spring/Summer, 1973. p. 13.

98. Hopper, Thomas. "Kids Have Feelings Too. . ." *Input* Vol. 1, No. 2, 1974. p. 3.

99. *Character Education Curriculum Teacher's Handbook.* San Antonio: American Institute for Character Education, 1974. pp. 16–18.

100. *Ibid.*, p. 17.

101. *Use of Time and Talents.* Teaching Unit from the Level E 5th Grade Teacher's Guide. The Character Education Curriculum. San Antonio: American Institute for Character Education, 1974. pp. 1–2.
102. Kohlberg, L., and Turiel, E. "Moral Development and Moral Education." *Psychology and Educational Practice.* (Edited by Gerald S. Lesser.) Glenview, Ill.: Scott Foresman and Co., 1971. p. 416.
103. *Ibid.,* p. 447.
104. See Rest, J.; Turiel, E.; and Kohlberg, L. "Relations Between Level of Moral Judgment and Preference and Comprehension of the Moral Judgment of Others." *Journal of Personality* Vol. 37, 1969. pp. 225–252.
105. Kohlberg and Turiel, *op.cit.*
106. See Beyer, Barry K. "Conducting Moral Discussions in the Classroom." *Social Education* Vol. 40, No. 4, April 1976. pp. 194–202, and Fenton, E.; Colby, A.; and Speicher-Dubin, B. "Developing Moral Dilemmas for Social Studies Classes." Unpublished paper for Moral Education and Research Foundation, Harvard University, 1974.
107. In Beyer, *op.cit.,* pp. 194–195.
108. Galbraith, R. E., and Jones, T. M., "Teaching Strategies for Moral Dilemmas." *Social Education* Vol. 39, No. 1, Jan. 1975. pp. 16–22.
109. Galbraith, R. E., and Jones, T. M. *Moral Reasoning: Teaching Strategies for Adapting Kohlberg to the Classroom.* Anoka, Minn.: Greenhaven Press, Inc., 1976.
110. Beyer and Fenton, Colby, and Speicher-Dubin, *op.cit.*
111. Simon, Frank. "Moral Development; Some Suggested Implications for Teaching." *Journal of Moral Education* Vol. 5, No. 2, 1976. pp. 173–178.
112. Craig, Robert Paul. "Education for Justice: Some Comments on Piaget." *Contemporary Education* Vol. 47, No. 2, Winter, 1976. pp. 69–73.
113. Kohlberg, with Whitten, *op.cit.*
114. Beck., *op.cit.*
115. *Ibid.* p. 2.
116. Mosher, R. L., and Sprinthall, N. A. "Psychological Education in Secondary Schools: A Program to Promote Individual and Human Development." *American Psychologist* Vol. 25, 1970. pp. 911–924.
117. Superka, and others, *op.cit.,* p. 55.
118. Hunt, M. P., and Metcalf, L. E. *Teaching High School Social Studies: Second Edition.* New York: Harper and Row, 1968. pp. 130–131.
119. Coombs, Jerrold R. "Objectives of Value Analysis." *Values Education: Rationale, Strategies, and Procedures.* (Edited by Lawrence E. Metcalf.) Washington, D.C.: National Council for the Social Studies, 1971. p. 19.
120. *Ibid.,* p. 20.
121. Coombs, J. R., and Meux, M. "Teaching Strategies for Value Analysis." *Values Education: Rationale, Strategies, and Procedures.* (Edited by Lawrence E. Metcalf.) Washington, D.C.: National Council for the Social Studies, 1971. pp. 29–74.

122. Their theory is discussed in these two books: Oliver, Donald, and Shaver, James P. *Teaching Public Issues in the High School*. Boston, Mass.: Houghton Mifflin, 1966.; Newmann, Fred M., with Donald W. Oliver. *Clarifying Public Controversy: An Approach to Teaching Social Studies*. Boston, Mass.: Little, Brown, 1970.

123. Massialas, Byron G., and Cox, C. Benjamin. *Inquiry in the Social Studies*. New York: McGraw-Hill, 1966.

124. Hunt and Metcalf, *op.cit.*

125. Fraenkel, Jack R. "Strategies for Developing Values." *Today's Education* Vol. 63, No. 7, Nov./Dec. 1973. pp. 49–55.

126. Superka, and others, *op.cit.*, pp. 55–56.

127. Coombs and Meux, *op.cit.*, pp. 30–31.

128. *Ibid.* p. 29.

129. Oliver and Shaver, and Newmann, with Oliver, *op.cit.*

130. Newmann, with Oliver, *op.cit.*, p. 43.

131. Oliver and Shaver, *op.cit.*, pp. 126–130.

132. Massialas and Cox, *op.cit.*

133. *Ibid.*, p. 166.

134. Hunt and Metcalf, *op.cit.*

135. *Ibid.*, p. 134.

136. Fraenkel, *op. cit.*

137. *Ibid.*, p. 49.

138. *Ibid.*

139. *Ibid.*, pp. 49–51.

140. *Ibid.*, p. 51.

141. Shaftel, Fannie, and Shaftel, George. *Role-Playing for Social Values: Decision-making in the Social Studies*. Englewood Cliffs, N.J.: Prentice-Hall, 1967.

142. *Ibid.*, p. 8.

143. *Ibid.*, p. 12.

144. *Ibid.*, pp. 65–66.

145. *Ibid.*, pp. 288–289.

146. Brown, George Isaac. *Human Teaching for Human Learning*. New York: Viking Press, 1971.

147. *Ibid.*, pp. 3–4.

148. Weinstein, G., and Fantini, M., editors. *Toward Humanistic Education: A Curriculum of Affect*. New York: Praeger, 1970.

149. Borton, Terry. *Reach, Touch, and Teach: Student Concerns and Process in Education*. New York: McGraw-Hill, 1970.

150. Shapiro, Stewart, B. "Developing Models by 'Unpacking' Confluent Education." *The Live Classroom: Innovation Through Confluent Education and Gestalt*. (Edited by George Isaac Brown.) New York: Viking Press, 1975. pp. 112–113.

151. Brown, George Isaac. "Human is as Confluent Does." *The Live Classroom: Innovation Through Confluent Education and Gestalt*. New York: Viking Press, 1975. p. 106.

152. Brown, George Isaac. *Human Teaching for Human Learning*. New York: Viking Press, 1971. pp. 41–42.

153. Cassarino, Anita. "Gestalt in the Second Grade: Merging of the Inner and Outer Worlds." *The Live Classroom: Innovation Through Confluent Education and Gestalt.* (Edited by George Isaac Brown.) New York: Viking Press, 1975. pp. 174–183.

154. *Ibid.*, p. 177.

155. Superka, and others, *op.cit.*, p. 177.

156. Barr, Robert D. "The Development of Action Learning Programs." *NASSP Bulletin*, May 1976. pp. 106–109.

157. Newmann, Fred M. *Education for Citizen Action: Challenge for Secondary Curriculum.* Berkeley, Calif.: McCutchan Pub. Co., 1975.

158. Graham, Richard. "Youth and Experiential Learning." *Youth: 74th Yearbook of the National Society for the Study of Education.* (Edited by Robert J. Havighurst and Philip H. Dreyer.) Chicago: University of Chicago Press, 1975. pp. 161–192.

159. *Ibid.*, p. 162.

160. *Ibid.*, pp. 181–183.

161. Superka, and others, *op.cit.*, p. 178.

162. Newmann, Fred M. "Student Intentions in Social Action Projects." *Social Science Education Consortium Newsletter.* No. 12, Feb. 1972. pp. 1–4.

163. *Ibid.*, p. 1.

164. Kirschenbaum, Howard. "Sensitivity Modules." *Humanistic Education Sourcebook.* (Edited by Donald A. Read and Sidney B. Simon.) Englewood Cliffs, N.J.: Prentice-Hall, 1975. pp. 315–320.

165. *Ibid.*, p. 316.

166. Allen, *op.cit.*, p. 63.

167. *Ibid.*, p. 61.

168. Sweeney, J. A., and Parsons, J. B. "Teacher Preparation and Models for Teaching Controversial Social Issues." *Controversial Issues in the Social Studies: A Contemporary Perspective.* (Edited by Raymond H. Muessig.) Washington, D.C.: National Council for the Social Studies, 1975. pp. 65–66.

169. Allen, *op.cit.*, pp. 61–67.

170. Curwin and Curwin, *op.cit.*, p. 79.

171. Porter, N., and Taylor, N. *A Handbook for Assessing Moral Reasoning.* Toronto, Ontario: Ontario Institute for Studies in Education, 1972.

172. Rest, J. R.; Coder, R.; Masanz, J.; and Anderson, D. "Judging the Important Issues in Moral Dilemmas—an Objective Measure of Development." *Developmental Psychology.* Vol. 10, No. 4, 1974. pp. 491–501.

173. Fulda, T. A., and Jantz, R. K. "Moral Education Through Diagnostic-Prescriptive Teaching Methods." *The Elementary School Journal.* May 1975. pp. 513–518.

174. Piaget, *op.cit.*

175. Sugarman, Barry. *The School and Moral Development.* London: Croom Helm Ltd., 1973. p. 7.

176. Dreeben, Robert. *On What Is Learned in School.* Reading, Mass.: Addison-Wesley Pub. Co., 1968.

177. Jackson, Philip. *Life in Classrooms*. New York: Holt, Rinehart, and Winston, 1968.
178. Spady, William G. "The Impact of School Resources on Students." *Review of Research in Education*. Itasca, Ill.: F. E. Peacock Pub. Inc., 1973. pp. 135–177.
179. Grannis, Joseph. "The School as a Model of Society." *Harvard Graduate School of Education Association Bulletin*. Vol. 12, No. 2, Fall 1967. pp. 15–27.
180. Hess, R. D., and Torney, J. V. *The Development of Political Attitudes in Children*. New York: Doubleday Anchor Book, 1968.
181. Beck, Clive, and Sullivan, Edmund V. "Moral Education in a Canadian Setting." *Phi Delta Kappan* Vol. 56, No. 10, June 1975. pp. 679–683.
182. *Ibid.*, p. 700.
183. Kohlberg, Lawrence. "The Cognitive-Developmental Approach to Moral Education." *Phi Delta Kappan* Vol. 56, No. 10, June 1975. pp. 670–677.
184. Scharf, Peter. "The Just School Concept." *Cutting Edge*, January 1976. pp. 16–23.
185. Kuhmerker, Lisa. "Dialogue: Edwin Fenton Talks with Lisa Kuhmerker". *Moral Education Forum* Vol. 1, No. 1, February 1976. pp. 1, 9–11.
186. Kohlberg, with Whitten, *op. cit.*, p. 212.
187. Kohlberg, *op. cit.*
188. Simon makes this statement in the forward to the *Search for Values*, written by Gerri Curwin, Rick Curwin, Rose Marie Kramer, Mary Jane Simmons, and Karen Walsh. Fairfield, N.J.: Cebco Standard Publishing Co., 1972. p. 8. Used by permission of the publisher.

Bibliography

GENERAL BIBLIOGRAPHY

Albert, Ethel M., and Kluckhohn, Clyde. *A Selected Bibliography on Values, Ethics, and Esthetics, in the Behavioral Sciences and Philosophy, 1920-1958.* Glencoe, Ill.: Free Press, 1959.

Nearly two-hundred references.

Bibliography on Education in Morals and Values, 1975. Available from Russell A. Hill, director, Planning for Moral/Citizenship Education, Research for Better Schools, Inc., 1700 Market Street, Philadelphia, Pa. 19103.

A collection of over 1,800 cited articles, books, and curriculum materials between 1960 and 1975.

Bouchard, L. A. M. and Bruneau, W. A., editors. *A Catalogue of Materials for Teaching and Research in Values Education.* Vancouver, British Columbia.: University of British Columbia, 1975.

Bouchard, L. A. M., and Burneau, W. A., editors. *Third Edition of Association of Values Education Research.* Vancouver, British Columbia: University of British Columbia, 1975.

Items are indexed by discipline, components discussed, and the nature of publications (2,500 entries).

Canfield, John, and Phillips, Mark. *Humanisticography* (originally published in *Media and Methods* Vol. 8 No. 1. September 1971.)

Annotated resource guide to over 130 books, films, tapes, simulations, classroom exercise books, curricula, journals, and organizations in the field of values and humanistic education.

Kelley, Marjorie. *In Pursuit of Values: A Bibliography of Children's Books.* New York: Paulist Press, 1973.

An annotated bibliography of books oriented for elementary, junior, and senior high schools which present moral dilemmas.

Kirschenbaum, Howard, and Glaser-Kirschenbaum, Barbara. *An Annotated Bibliography on Values Clarification,* 1973. Available from the National Humanistic Education Center, Springfield Road, Upper Jay, N.Y. 12987.

Contains a significant number of articles and books on values clarification since 1965.

Kuhmerker, Lisa. *A Bibliography on Moral Development and the Learning of Values in Schools and Other Social Settings.* New York: Center for Children's Ethical Education, 1971. ED 054 014.

Includes a wide selection of books and writings on moral development, values in education, psychological approaches to learning values, cultural approaches to learning values, and other related readings.

Moral and Values Education: Bibliographies in Education, No. 44. Ottawa, Ontario, Canada: Canadian Teacher's Federation, 1974. ED 097 269.

Books, articles, and theses from 1968–1973 (414 citations).

Morse, William C., and Manger, Richard L. *Affective Development in Schools: Resource Programs and Persons*, Fall, 1975. Available from Behavioral Science Education Project, Ann Arbor Community Services, Washtenaw County Community Mental Health Center, Ann Arbor, Mich.

Contains brief descriptions of diversive programs and approaches to values and affective education.

——————————. *Helping Children and Youth with Feelings*, Spring, 1975. Available from Behavioral Science Education Project, Ann Arbor Community Services, Washtenaw County Community Mental Health Center, Ann Arbor, Michigan.

An extensive bibliography which surveys the literature and materials in values and affective education.

Nicholson, Sandy. *Values, Feelings, and Morals: Part II: An Annotated Bibliography of Programs and Instructional Materials.* Washington, D.C.: American Association of Elementary/Kindergarten/Nursery Educatory, 1974. ED 095 472.

Refers to bibliographies, books, catalogues, media, and curriculum programs on affective and moral/values development of primary age children.

Rosenzweig, Linda N. "A Selected Bibliography of Materials about Moral Education Based on the Research of Lawrence Kohlberg." *Social Education*, Vol 40, No. 4, April 1976. pp. 208–212.

A good selection of introductory readings on leading moral discussions, sources for moral dilemmas, moral thought and action, philosophical principles of moral development, psychological principles of moral development, and the place of moral development in education.

Selective Bibliography on Valuing as an Educational Approach to Drug Abuse and Other High Risk Behaviors. 1975. Available from Drug Abuse Prevention Education Center, 1250 South Grand Avenue, Santa Ana, Calif. 92705, Herbert O. Brayer, coordinator, Orange County Department of Education.

Cites books, journal articles, research dissertations, project studies, tests and evaluation instruments, and classroom materials on teaching values.

Thomas, Walter L. *A Comprehensive Bibliography on the Values Concept,* 1967. ED 024 064 also available from Project on Student Values, Northview Public Schools, 3869 Plainfield, N.E., Grand Rapids, Mich. 49505.

Cites 800 articles and books dealing with values appearing after 1945.

SELECTED BIBLIOGRAPHY OF SUPPORTING
CURRICULUM MATERIALS

STUDENT MATERIALS (TEXTS)

About Me. Chicago; Ill.: Encyclopaedia Britannica Educational Corporation. Intermediate level.

Better Living Booklets. Chicago, Ill.: Science Research Associates. Titles include:

Self-Understanding: A First Step to Understand Children by W. W. Menninger.
Developing Responsibility in Children by Constance J. Roster.
Helping Children Develop Moral Values by Ashley Montagu.
Secondary level.

Campbell, David. *If You Don't Know Where You're Going You'll Probably End Up Somewhere Else.* Niles, Ill.: Argus Communications, 1974. Secondary level.

Can of Squirms. San Diego, Calif.: Pennant Educational Material. Separate editions for primary, intermediate, junior high, and high school.

Church, John G. *A Probe into Values.* New York: Harcourt Brace Jovanovich, 1973. Grades 4–6.

Cohen, J. *Value-Cards.* Pinellas Park, Fla.: Value Publishing Co., 1975.

Dating-Communication and Decision-Making. Minneapolis, Minn.: Winston Press. Grades 10–12.

Effective Personal and Career Decision-Making. Sunnyvale, Calif.: Westinghouse Learning Press. Senior High level.

Essence Cards - Essence I and Essence II. Menlo Park, Calif.: Addison-Wesley, 1971, 1975.

Exploring American Values (Education Development Center Bicentennial Project). Cambridge, Mass.: Education Development Center. Secondary level.

Fisher, Carl, and Linbacher, Walter. *Dimensions of Personality.* Dayton, Ohio: Pflaum/Standard, 1969, 1970, 1972. Titles are:

Let's Begin	*Here I Am*
Now I'm Ready	*I'm Not Alone*
I Can Do It	*Becoming Myself*
What About Me	
Grades K-6.	

Gelatt, H. B.; Varenhorst, Barbara; and Carey, Richard. *Deciding.* New York: New York College Entrance Examination Board, 1972. Junior High and High School level.

Gelatt, H. B.; Varenhorst, Barbara; and Miller, Gordon P. New York: *Decisions and Outcomes.* New York College Entrance Examination Board, 1973. Senior High and Junior College level.

Guidance Series Books. Chicago, Ill.: Science Research Associates. Titles are:

Becoming A Good Leader—Kenneth Wells
Building Your Philosophy of Life—T. V. Smith
Exploring Your Values—Mary Noff and Marilyn Pomer
Growing Emotionally—W. Walter Menninger
Understanding Yourself—W. Walter Menninger
What Is Honesty?—Thaddeus B. Clark
    Grades 7–14.

Hang-Up: The Game of Empathy. Madison, Wisc.: Educational Manpower, Inc. Grades 7–12.

Help: A Problem Solving Guide for Young People. Minneapolis, Minn.: Mine Publications. Junior High and Senior High grade levels.

How To Decide: A Guide for Women. New York: College Entrance Examination Board, 1975. Senior High grade level.

Howard, Robert. *Roles and Relationships: Exploring Attitudes and Values.* New York: Westinghouse Learning, 1973. Grade 12 - Adult.

Irwin, Karen, and Franklin, Susie F. *The Total Person.* San Diego, Calif.: Pennant Educational Material, 1976. Junior High level.-Adult. (game)

Kosuth, Joan, and Minnesang, Sandy. *Choices: A Guide for Organizing a Course in Personal Decision-Making.* San Diego, Calif.: Pennant Educational Material, 1975. Senior High level.

Life Skill Kits. Madison, Wisc.: Educational Manpower, Inc. Grades 7–12. (game)

Life Style-Values. Madison, Wisc.: Educational Manpower, Inc. Grades 9–12. (game)

Price, Roy. *Concepts for Social Studies.* New York. Macmillan, 1974. Titles are:

The Arena of Values
A Walk in My Neighbor's Shoes
The Crux of the Matter
The Cement of Societies
    Grades 9–12.

Riemer, George. *Dating: Communication and Decision-Making.* Minneapolis, Minn., 1975. Senior High level.

Silver, Michael. *Facing Issues of Life and Death.* St. Louis, Mo.: Milliken Publishing Co., 1976. Grades 7–12.

Student Value Setting. Clinton, Mississippi: J. B. Publishers. Intermediate grade level.

> *Value Questionnaires for Marriage and Family Living.*
> (Grades 11–12)
> *Value Questionnaires for United States Government.*
> (Grades 10–12).
> *Values Questionnaires for United States History.*
> (Grades 8–12).

Sun Valley, Calif.: Edu-game Creative Classroom Activities, 1975.

Whatever Happened to the Old-Fashioned Values? Chicago, Ill.: Curriculum Innovations, 1970. Senior High level.

You-Crisis Resolution Games. Madison, Wisc.: Educational Manpower. Grades 7–12. (game)

TEACHER MATERIALS (TEXTS AND GUIDES)

Allen, Rodney F. *Instructional Activities Series.* Oak Park, Ill.: National Council for Geographic Education, n.d. Titles are:

> *Environmental Education as Telling Our Stories*
> *This World Is So Beautiful: Feelings and Attitudes in Environmental Education*
> *But the Earth Abideth Forever: Values in Environmental Education.*

Dunfee, Maxine, and Crump, Claudia. *Teaching of Social Values in Social Studies.* Washington, D.C.: Association for Childhood Education International, 1974.

Gibson, John. *The Intergroup Relations Curriculum: A Program for Elementary School Education.* Vol. 2. Boston, Mass.: Lincoln Filene Center for Citizenship and Public Affairs, 1969.

Hawkins, ALice S., and Ojemann, Ralph H. *A Teaching Program in Human Behavior and Mental Health.* Cleveland, Ohio: Educational Research Council of America, 1970.

Heyer, Robert J., and Payne, Richard J., editors. *Discovery Patterns, Book 2: Dynamics and Strategies.* New York: Paulist Press, 1969.

Lipman, Matthew, and Sharp, Ann. *Instructional Manual to Accompany "Harry Stotlemeier's Discovery."* Upper Montclair, N.J.: Institute for the Advancement of Philosophy for Children, 1975.

113

Reichert, Richard. *Self-Awareness Through Group Dynamics.* Dayton, Ohio: Pflaum/Standard, 1970.

Schrank, Jeffrey. *Media In Value Education.* Niles, Ill.; Argus Communications, 1970.

——————. *Teaching Human Beings: 101 Subversive Activities for the Classroom.* Boston: Beacon Press, 1972.

Shaver, James P. *Facing Value Decisions: Rationale Building for Teachers.* Belmont, Calif.: Wadsworth, 1976.

Swenson, William G. *The Search for Values Through Literature.* New York: Bantam Books, Inc., 1973.

Todd, Karen Rohne Pritchett. *Promoting Mental Health in the Classroom: A Handbook for Teachers.* Rockville, Md.: National Institute of Mental Health, 1973.

Weiser, Conrad. *Dancing All the Dances, Singing All the Songs.* Philadelphia,Pa.: Fortress Press, 1975.

Weiser, Carol; Weiser, Conrad; and Miller, Charles. *Mix Me a Person.* Philadelphia, Pa.: Fortress Press, 1975.

FILMSTRIPS

The Adolescent Experience: Developing Values. New York: Guidance Associates. Grades 9–12. (two parts)

The Black and White Statue.
The Black Rabbits and the White Rabbits. Tarrytown, N.Y.: Schloat Productions. Intermediate and Junior High grade levels.

Career Values: What Really Matters to You. New York: Guidance Associates. (five parts)

Competitive Values: Winning and Losing. Pound Ridge, N.Y.: Human Relations Media Center. Junior High and Senior High grade level. (two parts)

Creative Values: Justice, Equality, Liberty. Tarrytown, N.Y.: Schloat Productions. Intermediate and Junior High grade level. (four parts)

Drugs, Values, and Personal Problems. Tarrytown, N.Y.: Schloat Productions. Secondary level. (six parts)

Exploring American Values: The Meaning of Equality. Pound Ridge, N.Y.: Human Relations Media Center. Junior High and Senior High grade level. (three parts)

Getting Along with Others. San Diego, Calif.: Pennant Educational Materials. Grades 5–8.

Law and Order: Values in Crisis. Tarrytown, N.Y.: Schloat Productions. Secondary level. (six parts)

The Punishment Fits the Crime. Tarrytown, N.Y.: Schloat Productions. Intermediate and Junior High grade level.

Science and Society: An Inquiry into Technology and Values. Tarrytown, N.Y.: Schloat Productions. Secondary level. (four parts)

Seeds of Hate: An Examination of Prejudice. Tarrytown, N.Y.: Schloat Productions. (two parts) Secondary level.

Understanding People. San Diego, Calif.: Pennant Educational Materials. Grades 5–8.

Values for Dating. Pound Ridge, N.Y.: Human Relations Media Center, 1974. (four parts)

Values for Teenagers in the 1970's. New York: Guidance Associates. Grades 9–12. (two parts)

What Are Your Values and Why. New York: *New York Times.* Secondary level. (six parts)

Wonderworm Values in Story and Song. San Diego: Calif.: Pennant Educational Materials. Elementary level.

MULTIMEDIA

Abby, David. *Valuing: A Discussion Guide for Personal Decision-Making.* Chicago, Ill.: Human Development Institute (Division of Instructional Dynamics, Inc.) Secondary level.

Anderson, Judith L., and others. *Focus on Self-Development.* Chicago, Ill. Science Research Associates, 1970. Elementary level.

Brandwein, Paul. *Self Expression and Conduct: The Humanities.* New York: Harcourt Brace Jovanovich, 1974–1975. Elementary level.

Carr, D. B., and Willenberg, E. P. *Teaching Children Values.* Freeport, N.Y.: Honor Your Partner Records, 1966. Elementary level.

The Center for Humanities, Inc. White Plains, N.Y.: These slide-cassette programs blend selections from novels, plays, poetry, popular songs, and film to encourage values clarification and decision-making. Two carousel slides, 2 records, and teacher's guidebook. Titles are:

Clarifying Your Values: Guidelines for Living

Conflict in American Values: Life Style vs. Standard of Living
Deciding Right from Wrong: Dilemma of Morality Today
Decision-Making: Dealing with Crises
Freedom and Responsibility: A Question of Values
The Ethical Challenge: Four Biomedical Case Studies
Hard Choices: Strategies for Decision-Making
Human Values in an Age of Technology
Man and His Values: An Inquiry into Good and Evil
The Origins of American Values: The Puritan Ethic to the Jesus Freaks.
Secondary grade level

Cromwell, Chester R. *Becoming: A Course in Human Relations.* Philadelphia, Pa.: J. P. Lippincott Co. Titles are:

Module I *Relating*
Module II *Interaction*
Module III *Individuality*
Secondary level.

Developing My Values; Child's World. San Diego, Calif.: Pennant Educational Materials. A set of 8 study prints. Elementary grade level.

Dinkmeyer, Don. *Developing Understanding of Self and Others.* Circle Pines, Minn.: American Guidance Service, 1970, 1973. Elementary grade level.

Educational Research Council of America. Cleveland, Ohio. Titles are:

Teaching Program for Education in Human Behavior and Potential. (K–6)
Curricula in Modern Programs for Youth (grades K-12)
Learning to Decide Program (grades 4–6)
Values and Commitment (K-5)
Values and Decision-Making Program (grades 7–10).

Hall, Brian. *Valuing: Exploration and Discovery.* San Diego, Calif.: Pennant Education Materials, 1971. Secondary level.

Patterns of Human Conflict. Tarrytown, N.Y.: Schloat Productions. Secondary level.

"Value Series" *Audio-tapes.* Baltimore, Md.: Media-Materials, Inc. Grades 6–9. Titles are:

Actions and Values
Recognizing Value Conflicts
Resolving Value Conflicts
Supporting Value Statements
What Are Values?

"Values Clarification Series" *Audio-tapes.* Baltimore, Md.: Media-Materials, Inc. Grades 6–9.

Values Series. Santa Monica, Calif.: Educational Media, 1972. Picture Cards. Grades 1–6.

Values: What's Important to You? Howard, Margaret (ed.) New York: Contact Unit from Scholastic Book Services, 1975. Secondary level.

FILMS

Association-Sterling Films. New York. *Let the Rain Settle It.*

Benchmark Films. Briarcliff Manor, N.Y. *Beauty Knows No Pain.*

Churchill Films, Los Angeles, Calif. *Climb.*

CRM Educational Films, Del Mar, Calif. "Conflict and Awareness: A Film Series on Human Values".

Encyclopaedia Britannica Educational Corporation. Chicago, Ill. Titles are:

Late for Dinner: Was Dawn Right?
Only Benjy Knows: Should He Tell?
The Lemonade Stand: What's Fair?
What Your Authority?
Where's Your Loyalty?
Who Needs Rules?

Media Five Films. Los Angeles, Calif. *Human Relations and School Discipline.*

King Screen Productions. Seattle, Wash. Titles are:

Is It Always Right?
Joshua in a Box
Just Like You

Pathescope Educational Films. New Rochelle, N.Y. *Law and Justice for the Intermediate Grades.*

Phoenix Films, Inc. New York. Titles are:

Kantutura
The Raft

Project Associates, Inc. Washington, D.C. *Is It Always Right to be Right?*

Pyramid Films. Santa Monica, Calif. *Why Man Creates?*

Stuart Reynolds Productions, Inc. Beverly Hills, Calif. *The Eye of the Beholder.*

Teleketics. Los Angeles, Calif. Titles are:

After the First	*Gym Period*
Check-In Time	*Let the Rain Set In*
Come Back	*Mother Tiger, Mother Tiger*
Family Encounter	*Nobody Important*
Father/Daughter	*Social Encounter*
First Year A.D.	*William*
Glass House	*With Just a Little Trust*

Wombat Productions. White Plains, N.Y. *Films That Reach*. Titles are:

Almost Everyone Does	*I Think*
Big Boys Don't Cry	*Lonnie's Day*
Claude	*Styles*
I Am	

Xerox Films. Middletown, Conn. *The Eye of the Storm.*

SELECTED JOURNAL ISSUES AND READINGS

American Personnel and Guidance Journal, Vol. 51, No. 9, May 1973. "Psychological Education: A Prime Function of the Counselor."

Counseling and Values, Vol. 18, No. 2, Winter, 1974. Issue on cognitive developmental moral education.

Counselor Education and Supervision, Vol. 14, No. 4, June 1975. "Personal Development Through Schooling." Norman A. Sprinthall, guest editor.

Educational Opportunity Forum, Vol. 1, No. 4, Fall 1969. Issue on "Psychological Humanistic Education."

History and Social Science Teacher, Vol. 11, No. 1, February 1975. Special issue on "Values and Moral Education."

The Humanist, Vol. 32, No. 6, Nov.-Dec. 1972. "Moral Education for Children."

The Monist, Vol. 58, No. 4, Oct. 1974. "The Philosophy of Moral Education."

Phi Delta Kappan, Vol. 56, No. 10, June 1975. "Moral Education."

Religious Education, Vol. 69, No. 2, March-April 1974. "The Open Society: Shaping Religions and Values."

Religious Education, Vol. 70, No. 2, March-April 1975. "Values and Education: Pluralism and Public Policy."

The School Guidance Worker, Vol. 31, No. 2, Nov.-Dec. 1975. "Moral/Values Education."

Social Education, Vol. 31, No. 1, Jan. 1967). "The Elementary School: Focus on Values."

Social Education, Vol. 35, No. 8, Dec. 1971. "Teaching Valuing: Elementary Education Supplement."

Social Education, Vol. 39, No. 1, Jan. 1975. "Moral Education: Learning to Weigh Human Values."

Social Education, Vol. 40, No. 4, April 1976. "Cognitive-Developmental Approach to Moral Education," Edwin Fenton, editor.

Theory into Practice, Vol. 14, No. 4, Oct. 1975. "Moral Education."

Viewpoints, Vol. 51, No. 6, Nov. 1975. "Education and Moral Development."

The Yearbook of the Canadian Society for the Study of Education. Vol. 2, 1975. "The Teaching of Values in Canadian Education," Dr. A. C. Kazepides, editor.

Barr, Robert, editor. *Values and Youth: Teaching Social Studies in an Age of Crisis.* Washington, D.C.: National Council for the Social Studies, 1971.

Barrs, Stephan, and others. *Values Education-A Resource Booklet.* Toronto, Ontario: Ontario Secondary School Teachers Federation, 1975.

Beck, Clive; Crittenden, B. S.; and Sullivan, E. V., editors. *Moral Education: Interdisciplinary Approaches.* New York: Newman Press, 1971.

Collier, Gerald; Wilson, John; and Tomlinson, Peter, editors. *Values and Moral Development in Higher Education.* New York: John Wiley & Sons, 1974.

Depalma, David, and Foley, Jeanne M., editors. *Moral Development: Current Theory and Research.* Hillsdale. N. J.: Lawrence Erlbaum Associates, Inc., 1975.

Dunham, Joe, coordinator. *Handbook of the Value Education Project.* Aurora, Ill.: Aurora College, 1975.

Educational Testing Service. *Moral Development.* Proceedings of the 1974 ETS Invitational Conference, Princeton, N.J.: ETS, 1974.

Jelinek, James John, editor: *The Teaching of Values.* Tempe, Ariz.: Third Yearbook of Arizona ASCD, 1975.

Kohlberg, Lawrence. *Collected Papers on Moral Development and Moral Education.* Cambridge: Harvard University Laboratory for Human Development, 1973.

_____. *Stages in the Development of Moral Thought and Action.* New York: Holt, Rinehart, & Winston, 1970.

Kohlberg, Lawrence, and Turiel, Elliot, editors. *Moral Development and Moral Education.* Cambridge, Mass.: Harvard University Press, 1971.

_____. *Moralization: The Cognitive Developmental Approach.* New York: Holt, Rinehart, & Winston, 1973.

_____. *Recent Research in Moral Development.* New York: Holt, Rinehart, & Winston, 1974.

Leeper, Robert R., editor. *Emerging Moral Dimensions in Society: Implications for Schooling.* Washington, D.C.: Association for Supervision and Curriculum Development, 1975.

Lickona, Thomas, editor. *Moral Development and Behavior: Theory, Research, and Social Issues.* New York: Holt, Rinehart, & Winston, 1976.

Meyer, John. *Aspects and Models of Values Education.* Burlington, Ontario: Values Education Ontario Centre, 1975.

_____. *Moral/Values Clarification: A Comparison of Different Theoretical Models.* Toronto, Ontario: Ontario Ministry of Education, 1975.

Meyer, John, editor. *Reflections on Values Education.* Waterloo, Ontario: Wilfrid Laurier University Press, 1976.

Meyer, John; Burnham, Brian; and Cholvat, John, editors, *Values Education Theory/Practice/Problems/Prospects.* Waterloo, Ontario: Wilfrid Laurier University Press, 1975.

Mischel, Theodore, editor. *Cognitive Development and Epistemology.* New York: Academic Press, 1971.

Overly, Norman, editor. *The Unstudied Curriculum: Its Impact on Children.* Washington, D.C.: ASCD, 1970.

Phillips, James A. Jr., editor. *Developing Value Constructs in Schooling: Inquiry into Process and Product.* Worthington, Ohio: Ohio Association for Supervision and Curriculum Development, 1972.

Purpel, D., and Ryan, K. A. *A Schoolman's Guide to Moral Education.* Berkeley, Calif.: McCutchan Publishing Corporation. (In press).

Read, Donald, and Simon, Sidney, editors. *Humanistic Education Sourcebook.* Englewood Cliffs, N.J. Prentice-Hall, 1975.

Simon, Sidney and Kirschenbaum, Howard, editors. *Readings in Values Clarification.* Minneapolis, Minn.: Winston Press, 1973.

Sizer, Nancy, and Sizer, Theodore. *Moral Education: Five Lectures.* Cambridge, Mass.: Harvard University Press, 1970.

Superka, Douglas P., and Johnson, Patricia L., with Ahrens, Christine. *Values Education: Approaches and Materials.* Boulder, Colo.: Social Science Education Corsortium, 1975.

Superka, Douglas P., and others. *Values Education Sourcebook: Conceptual Approaches, Materials Analyses, and an Annotated Bibliography.* Boulder, Colo.: Social Science Education Consortium, 1976.

Ubbelohde, Carl, and Fraenkel, Jack, editors. *Values of the American Heritage: Challenges, Case Studies, and Teaching Strategies.* 46th Yearbook. Washington, D.C.: National Council for the Social Studies, 1976.

PROJECTS, NEWSLETTERS, AND CLEARINGHOUSES

American Institute for Character Education
P. O. Box 12617
San Antonio, Texas 78212

Conducts seminars and workshops; writes curricula; publishes teacher training manuals; constructs and implements evaluation tools; and disseminates information.

Association for Values Education and Research (AVER)
Dr. William A. Bruneau, AVER
Faculty of Education
University of British Columbia
Vancouver, British Columbia
Canada V6T 1W5

Projects include experiments in moral education, annotations of research literature, computerized bibliographies and position papers.

California Association of Moral Education
Association Notes and Resources in Moral Education
Editor, Don Cochrane
Department of Social and Philosophical Foundations
School of Education
California State University
Northridge, California 91324

Center for the Exploration of Values and Meaning (CEVAM)
8463 Castlewood Drive
Indianapolis, Indiana 46250

Research leadership training and designing curricula in process of value and meaning.

Citizenship Development Program
Dr. Richard C. Remy, Director
Mershon Center
199 West 10th Avenue
Columbus, Ohio 43201

Citizenship decision-making instructional materials.

Confluent Education Development and Research Center (CEDARC)
P.O. Box 30128
Santa Barbara, California 93105

Provides training in confluent education to teachers and other helping professions.

Deliberate Psychological Education
Dr. Ralph Mosher, Director
Boston University
111 Cummington Street
Boston, Massachusetts 02215

Project in moral values and adolescent education through guidance.

Counselor Education and Adolescent Moral Education
Lois Erikson and Norm Sprinthall
College of Education
University of Minnesota
Minneapolis, Minnesota 55430

Program of Education in Human Behavior and Potential
Education Research Council of America
Rockefeller Building, Room 213
614 Superior Avenue, West
Cleveland, Ohio 44113

A program to help teachers, administrators, and other school personnel extend their understanding and appreciation of human behavior. Another aspect of the program involves teaching human behavior curricular materials, including where people get their ideas, attitudes, and values.

Journal of Moral Education
Pemberton Publishing Co. LTD.
88 Islington High Street
London NI-8EN, England

Carries research reports from America and England and articles on moral education programs at all educational levels. Only periodical entirely devoted to moral education. Published three times a year, $11.25.

Moral Education Curriculum Project
(supported by the National Endowment for the Humanities)
Co-Directors:

Robert T. Hall	John Davis
College of Steubenville	Bethany College
Steubenville, Ohio	Bethany, West Virginia

Develops teaching materials and programs for junior high school students.

Moral Education Forum
Dr. Lisa Kuhmerker, editor
221 East 72nd. St.
New York, New York 10021

A newsletter in moral education. Five issues published each year, $5. Features news on conferences on moral development and moral education and listings of relevant books, articles, and research papers, as well as information about experimental education programs and curricula with a strong value dimension.

Moral Education Project
Ontario Institute for Studies in Education
Department of History and Philosophy of Education
252 Bloor Street West
Toronto, Ontario
Canada

The Moral Education Project under the direction of Clive Beck and Ed Sullivan is concerned with research, evaluation, and teaching strategies in moral education and ultimate life goals.

Moral Education Research Foundation
Larsen Hall—3rd Floor
Harvard University
Cambridge, Massachusetts 02138

Staff at the Center conducts research and intervention programs in moral development, based on the work of Lawrence Kohlberg. Write for reprint articles on moral education, moral development, workshop announcements, and academic training.

National Humanistic Education Center
Springfield Rd.
Upper Jay, New York 12987

Publishes the *Humanistic Educators Network* (an occasional newsletter) and distributes brochures which describe workshops and publications in values clarification and humanistic education.

Pennant Educational Materials
4680 Alvarado Canyon Road
San Diego, California 92120

A resource center and publisher for materials in values education, affective education, and decision-making materials.

Philadelphia Center for Humanistic Education
8504 Germantown Avenue
Philadelphia, Pa. 19118

Offers workshops in values clarification, personalizing education, and open education, as well as a clearinghouse for many value education publications.

Project Change
Tom Lickona, Director
Department of Education
State University of New York
Cortland, New York 13045

Project in children's thinking and moral development.

Project Search
William Clauss, Humanities Division
New York State Department of Education
Albany, New York 12224

Discussion guide on valuing, interpersonal and interdisciplinary skills, research on moral development.

Research for Better Schools
Directors, Russell Hill and Marian Chapman
"Skills for Ethical Action and Instructional Program"
1700 Market Street, Suite 1700
Philadelphia, Pa. 19103

Oriented for grades 7–8 with emphasis upon the regard for values of self, others, and society.

Schools Council Moral Education Project
Peter McPhail
Department of Educational Studies
15 Norham Gardens
Oxford, England

A curriculum development project designed to involve students in the process of making decisions, resolving conflicts, and learning to care.

Sierra Project
Project director, Dr. John Whitely
Department of Social Ecology
University of California at Irvine
Irvine, California 92717

Curriculum development in moral and psychological education for college students.

Social Studies School Service
10000 Culver Blvd.
Department 73
Culver City, California 90230

Catalogues: *Religion/Philosophy/Values/Psychology: 1976 Catalogue.* A clearinghouse for a wide assortment of commercially available values education materials.

Teaching for Responsible Behavior
Orange County Department of Education
Herbert O. Brayer, coordinator
1250 South Grand Ave.
Santa Ana, California 92705

Project uses a values-oriented approach to the prevention of drug abuse.
Teacher training and family in-service workshops have been implemented.

Values Development Education Program
College of Education
213 Erickson Hall
Michigan State University
East Lansing, Michigan

Creation of a school just community and pre-in-service teacher education.

Values Education Centre
John Meyer, Director
2468 Glenwood School Drive
Burlington, Ontario
Canada L7R3SI

Offers technical assistance, demonstrations, and learning materials in
values education.

Values Education Newsletter: New Trends, Programs, Products, and Ideas
in Values Education
Values Education Publications
P.O. Box 4407
Stanford, California 94305

This is a monthly newsletter, $11 per year.

Values Education Project
Harris County Department of Education
Shirley Rose, Curriculum Consultant
6208 Irving Blvd.
Houston, Texas 77022

Project is funded to develop, field test, and evaluate values-based al-
cohol/drug education programs K-12.

Value Education Project
Joe Dunham, Coordinator
Aurora College
Aurora, Illinois

A K-8 district-wide (Aurora schools) project whose goal has been to assist
teachers in values education approaches, through workshops, consultation,
and distribution of values education materials.

Values Education/Citizen Education Project
Social Studies Curriculum Center
Ted Fenton, director
Carnegie-Mellon University
Pittsburgh, Pennsylvania

Project includes the development of a rationale for civic education, teaching techniques, and curriculum development focusing on the justice structure of the school.

Warborough Trust Research Unit
John Wilson, Director
Oxford University Department of Educational Studies
15 Norham Gardens
Oxford, England

This is a research and development organization set up to continue the work done under the Farmington sponsorship since 1965, in the area of moral and religious education. It is concerned with basic research, the production of materials, and supervision of various projects in moral education.

These acknowledgments are continued from page 4.

Diagram of the teaching process for teaching a moral dilemma, from *Moral Reasoning: Teaching Strategies for Adapting Kohlberg to the Classroom* by Ronald E. Galbraith and Thomas M. Jones. Copyright © 1976 by Greenhaven Press, Inc. Reprinted by permission of Greenhaven Press, Inc., 1611 Polk St., N.E., Minneapolis, Minn, 55413.

Human Teaching for Human Learning by George Isaac Brown. Copyright © 1971 by Viking Press. Excerpted with permission.

Humanistic Education, edited by Donald A. Read. Copyright © 1975 by Prentice-Hall, Inc. Excerpted with permission.

Inquiry in the Social Studies by Byron G. Massialas and C. Benjamin Cox. Copyright © 1966 by McGraw-Hill Book Company. Excerpted with permission.

The Live Classroom: Innovation Through Confluent Education and Gestalt, edited by George Isaac Brown. Copyright © 1975 by Viking Press. Excerpted with permission.

"Name Tag," "A Personal Coat of Arms," "Twenty Things I Love To Do," and "Values Voting." Reprinted by permission of Hart Publishing Company, Inc., from its copyrighted volume *Values Clarification: A Handbook of Practical Strategies for Teachers and Students* by Sidney B. Simon, Leland W. Howe, and Howard Kirschenbaum.

Phi Delta Kappan, Volume 56, June 1975. Copyright © 1975 by Phi Delta Kappa. Excerpted with permission.

Psychology and Educational Practice, edited by Gerald S. Lesser. Copyright © 1971 by Scott, Foresman and Company. Excerpted with permission.

Role-Playing for Social Values: Decision-Making in the Social Studies by Fannie Shaftel and George Shaftel. Copyright © 1967 by Prentice-Hall, Inc. Excerpted with permission.

School and Community, May 1972. Copyright © 1972 by the Missouri State Teachers Association. Excerpted with permission.

Search for Values By Gerri Curwin, Rick Curwin, Rose Marie Kramer, Mary Jane Simmons, and Karen Walsh. Copyright © 1972 by Cebco Standard Publishing Company. Excerpted with permission.

Social Education, Volume 40, April 1976. Copyright © 1976 by the National Council for the Social Studies. Excerpted with permission.

Social Science Education Consortium Newsletter, Number 12, February 1972. Excerpted with the permission of the Social Science Education Consortium, Boulder, Colorado.

"Taxonomy of interpersonal skills" from Microteaching for Affective Skills" by Mary and David Sadker. *The Elementary School Journal,* November 1975. Copyright © 1975 by The University of Chicago Press. Reprinted with permission.